AM I BLACK ENOUGH FOR YOU?

AM I BLACK ENOUGH

Indiana University Press
Bloomington & Indianapolis

Todd Boyd

FOR YOU?

Popular
Culture
From
the
'Hood
and
Beyond

The paper used in this publication meets
the minimum requirements of American
National Standard for Information Sci-
ences—Permanence of Paper for Printed
Library Materials, ANSI Z39.48–1984.

∞™

Manufactured in the United States of
America

Library of Congress Cataloging-in-
Publication Data

Boyd, Todd.
    Am I Black enough for you? : popular
culture from the 'hood and beyond / Todd
Boyd.
        p.   cm.
        Includes bibliographical references and
index.
        ISBN 0-253-33242-7 (alk. paper). —
ISBN 0-253-21105-0 (pbk. : alk. paper)
        1. Afro-Americans in popular
culture.   I. Title.
E169.04.B67   1997
305.896'073—dc20
                                        96-30365
    2 3 4 5 02 01 00 99 98 97

"We People Who Are Darker Than Blue."

To the Brothers who didn't make it

F. Lee Bailey: Do you use the word "nigger" in describing people?
Mark Fuhrman: No sir.
Bailey: Have you used that word in the past ten years?
Fuhrman: Not that I recall, no.
Bailey: You mean if you called someone a nigger you have forgotten it?
Fuhrman: I'm not sure I can answer the question the way you phrased it, sir.
Bailey: Are you therefore saying that you have not used that word in the past ten years, Detective Fuhrman?
Fuhrman: Yes, that is what I'm saying.
Bailey: And you say under oath that you have not addressed any black person as a nigger or spoken about black people as niggers in the past ten years, Detective Fuhrman?
Fuhrman: That's what I'm saying, sir.
Bailey: So that anyone who comes to this court and quotes you as using that word in dealing with African Americans would be a liar, would they not, Detective Fuhrman?
Fuhrman: Yes, they would.
Bailey: All of them, correct?
Fuhrman: All of them.
Bailey: All right. Thank you.

Contents

Preface

On September 30, 1995, I attended the premiere of Allen and Albert Hughes's second feature film, *Dead Presidents*. As the haunting sounds of Isaac Hayes's "Walk On By" filled the theater, I was moved by the film's enthralling, though depressing, conclusion. Larenz Tate's character, Anthony Curtis, rode off into the abyss that has prematurely claimed the lives of so many African American men, the penitentiary.

The following morning, I stood in the main office of the Critical Studies Department at the USC Cinema School with an assembled crowd of curious onlookers, only one other of whom was Black. We were all waiting on the outcome of a criminal case that had occupied the public mind for well more than a year, a case that had clearly come to stand for much more than whether or not a former football great had murdered his ex-wife and her unsuspecting friend.

As that now too familiar female voice stumbled over the name Orenthal on her way to announcing O.J. Simpson's acquittal on all murder charges, an air of tension clouded the room. The original curiosity that had filled the room had transformed into a quiet hostility. A real-life O.J. Simpson, in a case that existed somewhere between fact and fiction, had somehow escaped the fate that a fictional Anthony Curtis had been unable to avoid the night before.

Though the room was overcrowded, my eyes were drawn to Casandra, the departmental secretary, the other African American in the room. As if we were speaking some sort of silent language, we were pulled to each other amid the grunts and moans of disgust and disbelief that the others were exchanging, almost as if we weren't even in the room. Though this case was far more complicated than this moment and the aftermath would tell, it will somehow always be reducible to a smile or a frown, depending on where you were coming from.

As someone who is often accused of "intimidating" whites, I seldom have the opportunity to be afraid of anything myself. But that day, even I felt the need to watch my step. I didn't even want anyone to see me smile, for fear of being guilty by association. People with whom I had laughed on many occasions now seemed to dismiss my individuality and lump me in with those other "black people." Malcolm X used to ask, "What do you call a black man with a Ph.D.?" His answer was, "A nigger." That day I felt what he meant in the worst possible way. (Notice, that's "nigger" with an "-er," not an "-a." As you read, you will understand the difference.)

Am I Black Enough for You? is an attempt to explain why this reflexive smile crossed my face and what that smile was covering up inside. About two weeks later, as the fury over O.J. was still in full swing, Louis Farrakhan led the Million Man March on Washington, D.C. This while Colin Powell's autobiography, *My American Journey,* was a bestseller, and his potential bid for the presidency was still a strong possibility. With all of these events happening at the same time, it was obvious that the Black male, in multiple manifestations, was still an integral part of the fabric that defines America.

As I pondered these thoughts, I was taken back to the streets of Detroit. Walking through downtown one afternoon, I encountered a rather talkative gentleman who shouted over and over again this memorable phrase: "The Black man gonna rise again!" Thinking about these events in the fall of 1995, I couldn't help but wonder whether the prophecy from that man in downtown Detroit had been fulfilled.

TB
August 1996

Acknowledgments

As no work would ever come into being without the support of others, I find it important to acknowledge those people who have directly or indirectly influenced the thoughts in this book. I begin by thanking both sets of my parents, Edward and Mozelle Boyd and Bonnie and Willis Mosley, for providing me with broad exposure to the world at an early age and never allowing me to be satisfied with mediocrity. A special thanks to Daryl Fox and Robert Burgoyne for introducing me to the game. I would also like to reach back and thank Marion Holliday for giving me my first opportunities to speak, write, and think critically in public. Your support in those formative years has not been forgotten.

Special thanks to those readers who read early versions of this manuscript and provided much-needed commentary: Ken Shropshire, Ron Green, Herman Gray, John Sloop, and David James. I would also like to thank my colleagues and the students at the USC School of Cinema-Television for giving me the space to do my thing in a supportive environment. I would like to thank the following students for their assistance during various phases of this book: Marla Shelton, Hilary Neroni, Christine Acham, and Karen Voss. In addition, I would like to thank the staff at Indiana University Press, especially Joan Catapano, who, though she probably doesn't remember, expressed interest in my work as early as my first year in graduate school.

A special shout out to Rick Famuyiwa, who, even though he heard much of the same shit over and over again, kept coming back for more. People like you make the gig worthwhile. Continue to blow up the spot. Additional props to Patrick Smith, David Was, and Robert Hurst for helping me understand the intricate nuances of music and the music industry. You provided a direct link to music that has deeply influenced my writing. Stay up!

In closing, I'd like to thank all those who embrace pride and dignity, while continuing to eschew tomming and jeffing as a way of life.

The game is strong!

PEACE

Dead Man Walkin': Tupac's Journey into the Heart of Darkness

Friday the 13th of September 1996 proved truly unlucky for Tupac Shakur. When the rap artist/actor/Black man died that day in a Las Vegas hospital of complications from several gunshot wounds, Black popular culture and Black life in America registered another fatality.

I was never a fan of Tupac's. I always thought he was "perpetrating." A former roadie for the group Digital Underground, Tupac was always trying to represent himself as something he was not: hard. But sometimes those can be the worst ones. A cat with something to prove is indeed a dangerous thing.

I have heard all of the stories about Tupac's antics, having witnessed what seemed like his nine lives, but a bit of personal reflection best summarizes his life for me. Last October, in the midst of all the things I mention in the preface of this book, I moderated a panel hosted by the Black Filmmakers' Foundation, entitled "Black Film: Then and Now." "Then" referred to the Blaxploitation era. The guests included Ron O'Neal (Priest in *Superfly*) and Max Julien (Goldie in *The Mack*). They personified Black masculinity in their time. The audience on this day and the ongoing public fascination with this era would attest to that.

At the conclusion of this event, we decided to extend our particularly postmodern Black experience and journeyed to that landmark of Southern California Blackness, Roscoe's House of Chicken and Waffles. And guess who walked in? Only a day after being paroled, in came Tupac with his entourage, casting a collective silence over the place. His bodyguards were quick to showcase their automatic weapons, and his boys didn't hesitate to engage in the requisite ghetto behavior. Yes indeed, all eyes were truly on him!

Caught between the historical representation of Black masculinity and the contemporary version, I couldn't quite decide which was more authentic. Now I know. Tupac, like Easy E before him, made sure that we didn't make the mistake of assuming that his persona was simply fictional. Tupac was constantly offering his own version of the old B. B. King song that my father used to play: "Thug life ain't the best life, but it's my life."

Is there a heaven for a "G"? As Tupac said, "Only God can judge me now."

AM I BLACK ENOUGH FOR YOU?

Introduction: Representin' the Real

Possession is the motivation
that is hanging up
the goddamn nation
Looks like we always end up in a rut
I can't use it
Trying to make real
Compared to what?

—Les McCann and Eddie Harris, "Compared to What?"

One of my most vivid childhood memories Is the constant presence of neatly though conservatively dressed Black men in dark suits with bow ties, sporting closely cropped hair, or a "Quo Vadis," as it was called at the time. These men were of course members of the Nation of Islam who sold *Muhammed Speaks* from the street corners of downtown Detroit. Their polite manner of speaking and dignified appearance were always interesting to me, and I looked forward to encountering them, if for no other reason than that they would often refer to me, a little boy, as "Sir" or sometimes "young brother," terms of acknowledgment and respect that had lasting meaning.

I guess in hindsight I was impressed by their pride and dignity, the fact that they looked you straight in the eye when talking, that they did not scratch when they did not itch, that they did not laugh when things were not funny, and that they seemed to remain stoic at all times, regardless of the circumstances. They appeared fearless and the embodiment of what people now refer to as "hard."

Later on in life I began to understand why this was the case. As I learned about the Nation, or the Black Muslims as they were called in that day, it became clear that the reason for their stunning appearance was that the teachings of the Honorable Elijah Muhammed had given them the self-esteem that so many Black men are deprived of. While I have never been interested in being a Muslim, as their religious code of honor is unappealingly restrictive, the restoration of pride and dignity to their mostly male followers was laudable. Upon further investigation I discovered that many of the members of the Nation were ex-convicts or recovering substance abusers who found solace in this particular place.

Indeed, the Nation had established as its primary target for membership the neglected souls of our ghettoized society. These individuals are best summarized by Marx's description of the lumpenproletariat or, more concisely, what Frantz Fanon later described as the "wretched of the earth." Considering the fact that so few people are truly interested in assisting these depressed and deprived individuals, I have to commend the Nation for their assistance, even though I still have problems with their overall beliefs.

This "respect" for the Nation of Islam eventually led me to write a chapter of my doctoral dissertation on their current leader, Louis Farrakhan, and his place in popular culture and political discourse. At the time I was interested in finding a strident aesthetic of Blackness, somehow related to Black nationalism, but updated from its last incarnation in the late 1960s and early 1970s. I innocently called what I was searching for "Afrocentricity." Since that time the notion of an Afrocentric discourse has all but disappeared from my thought process. This is due to a lived politics of location that not only informs what I write but, in essence, defines the subject.

When I started the project, I was finishing my graduate studies at the University of Iowa, and upon completion I worked at my first academic job, as a professor at the University of Utah. The placement of a Black man in either one of these settings would be bad enough, but together, one behind the other, they were certainly a feat deserving of additional compensation. I have often called this my "fly in the buttermilk" tour. Nonetheless, my thoughts during that time were indicative of being marginalized in a sense that I am sure most cultural theorists have never thought of. Thus my writing was in defense, a justification for African

American culture, as opposed to dealing with any substantive matter. While this process proved a good exercise, it was ultimately draining. African American culture does not need to be defended, as its impact on American culture is undeniable.

So as I began rethinking these ideas in the contested spaces of Los Angeles, I slowly realized that the battle lines were drawn somewhat differently. Here there was no doubt about the presence of African American culture; the point of reference had to do with its reception. I can vividly recall a member of the interview team at USC asking me to justify my critical inquiry into Louis Farrakhan. In the interviewer's mind, anything short of a pure dismissal was unacceptable. Not only was this attitude counterproductive in a scholarly environment, but as the public reaction after the October 1995 Million Man March would demonstrate, the refusal to treat the issue of Louis Farrakhan seriously remains a problem in American society. This dismissive attitude is still prevalent as I am writing this preface: one-time presidential hopeful Governor Pete Wilson of California in the spring of 1995 led a vote by the University of California Board of Regents to end affirmative action. Wilson and others, including the interviewer, want to dismiss Black people in a way much more direct than a simple critical dismissal, though.

I moved to L.A. shortly after a jury in Simi Valley tried to disregard the fact that several police officers, who are charged with upholding the law, decided that they were above that law in their beating of Rodney King. I was a true resident of L.A. by the time a second jury conceded the bare minimum in sentencing two of the officers, though a judge decided that their punishment was too severe.

By then it was no longer a novelty to see members of the Nation of Islam standing on the corner of Crenshaw and Vernon selling newspapers and beanpies, nor was it a rarity to see Black men and women dressed in Afrocentric garb as I traveled around the area where USC is situated. No, these things were no longer abstract intellectual concerns, as they were in Iowa or Utah, but real live artifacts that were not as romantic or as distant as my state of denial might have made them seem before moving to L.A.

What was real was the way in which I often oscillated between being surrounded by the gang members of South Central and the Hollywood "niggaz" with whom most of my social time was being spent. I was constantly transposed between the "gangstaz" that Ice Cube rapped about, and the "gangstaz" themselves—or for that matter Ice Cube himself. Black men were once again real, as they had been for so much of my life. Thus I had to approach my subject with the same determination with which I would approach a real Black man. Romanticized theoretical concepts would no longer be privileged over real interaction.

In all this, my subject matter began to change. No longer was I searching for an Afrocentric position in Black popular culture. Instead I was in search of what held these competing tenets together: how Black men navigated the treacherous terrain of L.A., and how my own identity was being transformed in the process. No longer was I the novelty image; I had become real as well.

My move to L.A. also underscored another reason why Afrocentricity no longer seemed a relevant concern. This new evaluation of Afrocentricity had to do with commodification at the highest level. In Hollywood, where commercialization is so deeply ingrained, the selling out of Black political discourse in popular culture was readily evident—not only in the way that numerous individuals wore Afrocentric clothing for style, though having little knowledge of the politics, but in that the whole political process seemed empty. The media had simply found a way of co-opting everything, from the picture of Malcolm X on Roc's wall, to the emblematic X on baseball caps. Nothing appeared to be sacred.

Though Hollywood and commodity have never been enemies, there was a time when culture and politics that deviated from the mainstream were viewed as threatening. When there was a political theme that ran through popular culture, it was bounded by the real-life threat of a strong political presence. For instance, Les McCann and Eddie Harris's challenging political tune "Compared to What" was informed by the fact that the Black Panther Party was asking some of the same questions in society. Whereas politics at one time prompted popular culture, now popular culture exists in a world where politics has been completely displaced. Politics can exist only to the extent that it is replicated in the media, and even then this is short-lived.

This began to occur to me while listening to Gil Scott-Heron shortly after the riots in the spring of 1992. His tune "The Revolution Will Not Be Televised," is a concise deconstruction of the uselessness of media in a world where the people have decided to address their fate. Media, in this construction, would be obsolete. They could in no way alter the demands of history. Yet in 1992 the revolution was televised, and it proved quite entertaining at that. Not only did it displace Cosby, but the prevalence of home video cameras proved that we no longer had to be satisfied with a dominant version of the news, either. Most of the best footage came from amateur filmmakers, whose street ethnography became more valuable than the normally sophisticated news crews and their footage. The revolution was televised, and the availability of video equipment at the personal level made it that much more of a media event. Up close and personal took on an entirely different meaning.

So with the need for more and more authentic footage, the people in the street became simultaneously their own best friend and worst enemy. On one hand, they used the instruments of technology to momentarily halt their own materially motivated rampage through the streets, or in some cases to demonstrate it. On the other hand, they functioned as their own publicist by foregrounding their own images, totally ignoring, while ultimately falling into, the same traps that the mainstream media normally set for impoverished minorities. Is this what Buggin' Out, the character in Spike Lee's *Do the Right Thing*, meant when he said, "Put some brothers on the wall"?

What we saw in those streets was a true expression of urban politics in the postmodern world. All pretense toward social revolution was displaced by the more immediate goal of accumulating the commodities that were often advertised but normally denied to these oppressed people. Watching this and the cultural events that followed showed me that this was the state of contemporary politics for the urban poor: the imitation of crass materialism, by any means possible. This made me realize that we had entered a new day, when chaos as a way of life was forced onto the mainstream agenda for the first time. So any attempt on my part to argue about the politics of popular culture as it was linked to any overriding ideological theme, particularly Afrocentricity, would be a total waste of time.

As far as cultural representations of African Americans are concerned, we are in a seller's market. As mainstream representation requires more and more images to fill the ever-expanding visual space, it is inevitable that there will be a minority presence. Though the overall control of the media lies in the hands of the real "other," I would be remiss if I did not point out that African Americans do have some control over their image. Considering that excess sells in general, the more excessive the African American image, the stronger the likelihood that it will be accepted. The politics of negotiated conformity, focusing on excess, dominates the representation of contemporary Black popular culture. For this reason, Snoop Doggy Dogg is more relevant today than Spike Lee. The focus in this text is the why and how of these present circumstances.

There is an interesting moment in the 1995 rap documentary *The Show* when Andre Harrell, current CEO of Motown, describes the difference between an earlier generation of rappers and today's version. Harrell, who in the early 1980s was part of the little-known rap group Dr. Jeckyl and Mr. Hyde, was discussing the group's moniker from that period, "The Champagne of Rap." In explaining the name, Harrell suggested that the members of his group were what he called "affirmative action" rappers, young men nurtured under the guise of upward social mobility. Thus champagne, and the class connotations that it implies, perfectly represented their ideological disposition. Harrell's description is enhanced when he begins to comment on the genre of gangsta rap. He states that gangsta rappers grew up in a different era and thus were what he called "Reaganomic" rappers, clearly suggesting that they had come under the influence of the harsh economic and social policies of Reagan/Bush, and that this not only separated them from a previous generation of rappers, but also tainted their view of the world forever, in a very specific way.

The transition from "affirmative action" rappers to "Reaganomic" rappers is a perfect metaphor for the issues covered in this book. What are the political, cultural, and economic shifts that separate two seemingly close groups into distinct generations? And how do these issues affect the culture that is produced?

In relation to Black popular culture, we have seen the results of two generations, one defined by the political struggles of the civil rights and Black Power movements, and the other defined by the political victimization of oppressed people for whom the American dream has truly become a nightmare, far surpassing anything that Michael Myers, Jason, or Freddy Kruger could ever perpetrate on film.

I make these points to emphasize what it means to analyze Black male culture in the context in which it is being produced. While the West Coast is not known for its intellectual acumen, it is known for the vast entertainment complex that produces the culture we all consume. "Hollywood" is the generic term that we often associate with this mode of production and the ensuing discourse that it brings. Considering all this, I am confronted with the task of being intelligent with respect to Black culture, while being an integral part of it. Those on the cultural side say that there is no meaning to what they do, that their work is often misinterpreted. They denounce both cause and effect. The academic side says that there is much meaning being produced, that cause and effect are parts of larger cultural systems, and that these cultural producers are simply agents of a much larger process. In Hollywood one has to listen to both sides. The writing in this book is a demonstration of these two approaches.

The entertainment world generally has little regard for academic pontification. The academic world, on the other hand, has much regard for entertainment, yet in such a distanced way that seldom do the twain meet. This book is an attempt to bring them together. Being that I get paid for academic pontification—though some find it entertaining that a Black man could do such a thing—I will begin by explaining how I see my position in this larger arena.

As cultural critics, we should aim to explain the various processes of culture in relation to aesthetics, the economy, and the political systems that define the larger world around us. Our goal is much like that of the country preachers I used to hear as a child who would be encouraged by a church member to "make it plain!" In the process of making it plain, we have to evaluate and deconstruct our subjects so as to speak to others about our interpretation of the material. So often, though, we make it plain only for the already converted, the huddled masses of other academics in our respective fields. We make it plain to people who already understand. This is a problem. There are so many people outside the academy who never read our books, attend our conferences, or take our classes. Yet these people are often more interesting to talk to and learn from than those of us who are supposedly educated.

This propensity toward isolation in academia is currently being challenged by a new generation of African American scholars who have internalized the fundamentals of the academy, but have chosen to pitch their ideas to a larger audience. Unfortunately, there are still many in the academy who assume that by being accessible, one is somehow less serious. As Black intellectuals gain a stronger foothold in the market-place, however, such pronouncements are becoming common. Often this debate is placed in the opposition between the terms "journalism" and "scholarship," the former clearly being less substantial than the latter. Thus, Black public intellectuals are considered journalists, while those intellectuals who deal in esoterica are considered scholars, and in some way use knowledge, like a country club membership, as an exclusionary resource. At the end of the day we must ask ourselves, Who does this help, and who does it hurt?

This dichotomy is similar to the old racially coded debate in sports that describes African American athletes as "natural" and white athletes as "hard-working." It is assumed that African American athletes are born with the skills to play and excel at sports, a clear reference to an assumed physical prowess that defies mental capacity, while white athletes are regarded as industrious, in keeping with the ideology of the American work ethic (see chapter 5). In the same way, it is assumed that Black scholars are somehow less well equipped, or as former Los Angeles Dodger general manager Al Campanis once said, they do not have the "necessities" to do the job.

These concerns are representative of the racism that is operative in code words offered by liberal whites in the form of a compliment that is really defined by traditional racist tenets being expressed in a new era.

African American cultural criticism has more to do with a mission of access to a large enough audience that the words can possibly mean something to the world in which we live, than with any lack of necessities. This is especially true when you consider that the academic credentials of African American cultural critics are indeed valid, if for no other reason than that they were earned according to the rules set in place by an overwhelmingly white academy.

It is my intention to fuse the formal and the vernacular in such a way that it informs both sides, as opposed to being limited to one or the other. As African American discourse has always been defined in conjunction with its audience, so too will be the scholarship that emanates from this position. Those African American scholars who are redefining the academy are like the African American musicians who constantly redefined American music throughout the twentieth century. They are forces that must be dealt with in the same way that blues, jazz, soul, and now rap must be dealt with. The key is being accessible without losing one's critical edge—to, in the immortal words of George Clinton, "dance underwater and not get wet."

If living in L.A. has taught me one thing, it is that entertainment sells, esoterica does not. Many would consider my stance to be a sellout. So as not to be misunderstood, let me say that insights on culture should be arrived at with nothing less than rigorous detail to attention. What I am suggesting, though, is that the work of scholars who make a living dealing with popular culture should in some sense be concerned with the popular in all its manifestations.

The model for this sort of project is Miles Davis and his legendary album *Kind of Blue* (1959), not only one of the most popular albums in jazz history, but one of the most progressive musical expressions of all time. Miles did not have to sacrifice quality to attract a large cross-section of the mass audience. Even people who have no real interest in jazz own *Kind of Blue.* The tunes from this album are easily recognizable to the most knowledgeable jazz purist and the jazz novice as well. In the same way, African American cultural critics must reach the academic purist as well as the casual reader who is interested in those things that exist beyond his or her immediate surroundings. What I am asking may simply be a pipe dream, a fantasy in a world where reality rules. This effort could very easily go down the same path of disappointment that Miles ended up on when he made *Water Babies* and *On the Corner*: a popular audience which was clearly listening to other things. Yet, in contrast to Miles's situation, there are several predecessors who can assist in this endeavor.

Recently the media have become interested in what are now called "public intellectuals"—all of whom, interestingly enough, have been

Black. Since the beginning of 1995, several major publications have commented on the emerging Black intellectuals who seem to be taking the academy by storm. Among others, the *New Yorker, Atlantic Monthly, Village Voice*, and *Los Angeles Times Magazine* have done cover stories on the Black intellectual in the 1990s. Names which continually pop up are Henry Louis Gates Jr., Cornel West, bell hooks, Houston Baker, and Michael Eric Dyson. These names have been bandied about in both positive and negative ways in sectors normally off-limits to academics. This popularity is coupled with a rise over the last five years in the number of publications by Black authors who study popular culture. At least for the time being, Black academics are in the mix. So the path has already been trod. Now is the time to till some new ground.

One of the most prevalent themes that inform the field of cultural studies, especially popular culture, is the tendency toward politicizing the objects we study. It is as though our interest in things that other people consider frivolous is somehow justified by the political dimension that we bring to them. Yet I have long had a problem with the phrase "popular culture," as there seems to be a hierarchy with respect to those things that we choose to study. The artifacts that receive the most attention are those that carry the most obvious progressive political baggage. If ever the demands of political correctness were a factor, it is in the study of popular culture. Why have I never read an intense study of the films of Rudy Ray Moore, the novels of Iceberg Slim or Donald Goines, the music of Tyrone Davis, etc.? Why? Because they do not fit in so easily with what we consider acceptable, and because they are works of the lower class that have never transcended the world of folk culture in which they exist. In addition, their politics are a huge stumbling block in light of the resulting contradictions. Nonetheless, they still need to be studied.

This is also true of contemporary culture. Though several people make cursory mention of rap music, few fully explore its possibilities. Those who do seem interested only to the extent that they can make rap into an artifact of political discourse. I am not suggesting that rap transcends this political dimension, but rather that it is a product of political circumstances in America; it is a defense of and a response to certain historical and social conditions. It need not be defended, though it is constantly under attack; its presence signifies a defense that can come only from the product itself.

As academics, we need not defend rap, though the pressures of intellectual life and the superstructure of the university profession strongly urge us to do so. As practitioners of culture studies, we are encouraged to find the political as a way of linking us with an academic community—e.g. Marxist, poststructuralist, feminist. Without these labels we are constantly dismissed, our work disregarded. And notice that this is the reaction that we receive from the so-called left side of the academic spectrum. So the pressure is on to do a Marxist reading of Ice Cube, or a feminist reading of Salt n Pepa, so as to prove to our colleagues that we are one with them, that we are ultimately no threat. We are like Rodney King, in that we want only to get along.

This book is an attempt to move beyond what I see as the constraints that define the study of contemporary African American culture. Though you will find the influence of both Marxist thought and poststructuralist discourse in my work, I consider myself a follower of neither. In addition, I must constantly remind myself not to fall into the trap of articulating a Black nationalist party line. Criticism, like the best of the jazz tradition, should be an improvisation on cultural studies itself. Though I may borrow from the intellectual styles mentioned earlier, it is the context in which the thoughts arise that propels the project. The art of improvisation is informed by many components but driven by one, an abiding notion of African American oral culture and its effects. In the same way, the improvisers of jazz nuanced existing meanings, while on the bandstand their primary function was the articulation of the oral impulses that have always defined Black life in America. In this process it is the appropriation of other forms and their usefulness in furthering the African American oral project.

Thus quotations are used as just that, quotes, appropriated thoughts that strengthen my points. This is similar to rappers' use of sampling, where preexisting forms of music are incorporated into the contemporary as a way of enhancing the overall project. As with improvisation, the original is useful not as an object of sacred devotion but as a way of motivating contemporary expression. In this process, the improviser and the sampler are judged on their ability to recontextualize, not on their acumen in imitating the original.

In jazz you are required to improvise, to create your own form of expression by using other bits of information as they inspire you. The emphasis is not on the original but on one's own articulation. In this way jazz and rap are very similar. As jazz improvises, rap emphasizes the freestyle, an impromptu lyrical explosion that is defined by its spontaneity. These are the oral forms I hope to express through my writing, to improvise on the canon of popular culture and freestyle my way through the idiom of African American life in the late twentieth century, doing both at the same time, without missing a beat.

This book is generally concerned with the expression of a distinct "ghetto mentality" as it informs some of the most contested forms of contemporary Black popular culture. My argument is that there is a specific form of Black cultural expression that emanates from those who are most oppressed by the conditions of postindustrial America and by years of systemic race and class subordination. The voice of the truly disadvantaged, or what I will identify as the sentiments associated with a metaphor defined as the "nigga," is not necessarily new, but is an expression that is specific to the conditions of impoverished urban America of the late 1980s through the 1990s. These concerns are intended to fill in the gap about African American life, which has been omitted from or ignored by more popular discussions of "Generation X," a phrase almost exclusively linked to white youth culture.

I have divided my inquiry into five segments of cultural production. In each case I discuss the cultural circumstances that define the production as well as the way in which the subjects of my inquiry articulate their position, in relation to both race and class.

The first chapter is concerned with the historical currents that have underlain the popular expression of African American culture, beginning in the mid-1980s with Bill Cosby and the popularity of *The Cosby Show*, regarding discussions of his "positive" image in the media. From there I move to the second phase, which highlights filmmaker Spike Lee and his prominent image in relation to African American film as a venue of cultural expression, and also to a renewed discussion of Black nationalist politics in culture. Finally, I move on to the most recent form of expression, which is most obviously foregrounded as a result of the mass popularity of the genre of gangsta rap. In each case I chart the politics of the movement and discuss why the preceding movements eventually succumb to the success and failure of gangsta rap and its influence in other areas of popular culture.

Following the historical background, I provide several separate accounts of how this idea of a "ghetto mentality" takes hold of the popular imagination. Chapter 2 looks at the split in political discourse between the Afrocentric politics of the rap group Arrested Development and the rejection of political discourse through a simultaneous embrace of Nation of Islam ideology and gangsta politics, both of which reflect lower-class sentiments about the more middle-class appropriation linked to Afrocentricity. In this regard, rapper and film star Ice Cube marks the dividing line between middle-class and lower-class politics.

Chapter 3 focuses on the rejection of a political agenda altogether as gangsta rap begins to become a true force in popular culture. This chapter demonstrates how the West Coast, especially the articulation of Blackness in Los Angeles, informs this nihilistic attitude toward both free expression and daily life.

Chapter 4 is similarly concerned with the gangsta ethos and the expression of nihilism, but in this case specifically with the way in which this phenomenon has influenced the political and visual dimensions of race and class through the cinema, especially John Singleton's amazingly popular *Boyz n the Hood* and Allen and Albert Hughes's *Menace II Society.* Chapter 5 looks at how these class politics have been expressed in an often overlooked area (though one of substantial importance), professional basketball, while openly exploring the importance basketball has had in Black popular culture relative to contemporary society. Finally I touch on the many popular concerns and contradictions surrounding this recent form of expression, offering alternative ways of understanding culture that emerge from the 'hood. In highlighting the commonly accepted problems of this culture, I also demonstrate the societal Catch 22 that these problems are a product of.

My study uses the Black male as a cipher in understanding the social fabric of contemporary American society. This book is an attempt to combine the nuances of African American oral expression— e.g., rap music, basketball—with critical insight into the culture that has been used to define Blackness as a form of being, and in turn to look at how Blackness has defined American popular culture.

Real Niggaz Don't Die: Generational Shifts in Contemporary Black Popular Culture

Just another Black man caught up in the mix
Tryin' to make a dollar outta fifteen cents.

—Tupac Shakur, "I Get Around"

When Tupac commented on the plight of the Black man in contemporary society, his implications were not lost. Instead of discussing Black masculinity in its most extreme form, Tupac measured the arduous task of being Black and male in America in its generality. We are, indeed, Black men caught up in a mix that is often confusing, even to those of us who study these sorts of things for a living.

The overriding sentiment has to do with the difficulty of trying to make "a dollar outta fifteen cents," or as the colloquial phrase has often signified, trying to run through hell in gasoline drawers—the chances of getting burned increase substantially with every step. In other words, trying to do the impossible on a regular basis, trying to exist in a world where you have always known that you were not wanted. Yet as we move deeper and deeper into the postindustrial era, we find that the world that once defined our labor as necessary, having changed substantially, no longer needs us either.

In many ways what Tupac was saying is no different from what Curtis Mayfield said in the early 1970s—that Black men are constantly "trying to get over." And as the hustler's ethos tends to define much of Black male life, we can understand why the simplest things tend to become complex with respect to the endangered and embittered African American male.

Yet even with the changes in American society in the last thirty years, the most strident Black male figures have always found some outlet of expression via popular culture. I am convinced that were it not for popular culture, Black men, especially lower-class Black men, would have worn out their welcome long ago. It is this role as the ultimate purveyors of popular culture, always providing the excitement, angst, irony, tension, and comic relief that are needed to sustain any cultural movement, that has kept Black men in the mix when all indicators suggest that they should have been extinct many years previous.

The plight of Black men simply trying to exist motivates much of what constitutes the strength of American popular culture. This existence is often expressed in ways that remind all who are listening of the impact and depth of Blackness, a continual presence regardless of the societal situation.

> Niggaz always gotta show they teeth
> Now I'mo be brief
> Be true to the game.
>
> —Ice Cube, "True to the Game"

Ice Cube's emphatic demand that one stay "true to the game" has to do with cultural authenticity and in some way furthers Tupac's meditations on the everyday struggle. Not only must one exist in a hostile world, but as the lure of financial and material success becomes real and the temptation to assimilate becomes stronger, it is necessary to remain true to one's cultural identity while existing in the mainstream. This is what is meant when rappers say, "Keep it real." Authenticity becomes a central issue.

Those who have embraced the strongest sense of cultural authenticity have held the longest-lasting influence over the culture at large. It is the strength of this cultural authenticity, which is challenged but never fully compromised by material possessions, mainstream recognition, or personal aggrandizement, that sets the contributions of certain Black males apart from those of cultural producers who simply get by on their pop appeal rather than really enhancing the culture.

In response to an interview question by bell hooks, Ice Cube suggests that the importance of certain elements of Black popular culture lies in a refusal to accommodate audiences, though they may be offended. "I feel that I've gotten the most success by not compromising. And I say it in interviews, that I do records for black kids, and white kids are basically eavesdropping on my records. But I don't change what I'm sayin'" (hooks and West, *Outlaw Culture*, 129). Ice Cube's idea of "eavesdropping" sheds light on why gangsta rap is so popular among white teenagers, but it also suggests that there are those who resist compromise and have the ability to provide a much more empowered, or at least more culturally significant, product than those who always go along with the compromises of the mainstream.

I am not suggesting that there is a pure and innocent Black male culture that supersedes the compromises of contemporary society, as there are several kinds of compromise that are integral to American corporate culture. I am arguing for a cultural space that is defined by those who use their complete disregard for the dictates of society and overall nonconformity to strengthen their cultural articulation.

> Charlie Parker? Charlie Parker. All the hip white
> boys scream for Bird. And Bird saying, "Up
> your ass, feeble-minded ofay! Up your ass."
> And they sit there talking about the tormented genius
> of Charlie Parker. Bird would've played not a note
> of music if he just walked up to East Sixty-seventh
> Street and killed the first ten white people he saw.
> Not a note!
>
> —Leroi Jones, *The Dutchman*

The true measure of all cultural producers is the contribution, residual impact, and substantive change that they leave with the culture they exist in. Charlie Parker, Miles Davis, Marvin Gaye, Muhammad Ali, and Richard Pryor contributed the combination of brilliance and tragedy at the core of what it means to be a Black man in America. Like the best jazz improvisers on the bandstand, these Black men have turned life's mundane moments into intellectual property of the highest order and made life's most difficult situations seem like the proverbial drop in the bucket. When Martin Luther King Jr. said that "truth crushed down to the earth will rise again," this is what he meant.

The work of each of these individuals evolved from the most entrenched forms of the Black oral tradition, and each used his knowledge of the tradition to inform the masses. In other words, each had what we now refer to as "crossover" appeal, but none of them "sold out," as it were, because Black culture and Black audiences were still their primary focus. They all remained true to the game, but in each case were subsumed by mainstream culture without a compromise on their part with respect to their cultural awareness, nor did they feel the need to cater to any sector of their audience in the process. In some ways, we could say that this refusal to "sell out" increased their frustration by exacerbating their personal demons and resulted in the self-destructive nature of their lives, and in many case the destruction of others close to them as well. Nonetheless, their fundamental impact on culture cannot be denied. They personified the popular phrase "stay Black," only to be victimized by it.

> I don't want to perform for white people. I'm not here to perform for them. I'm not here to show them I'm better. You get more respect from the "liberals" and the intelligent white people when they know you don't give a damn.
>
> —Allen Hughes, in Gates, "Blood Brothers"

What contemporary figures embody similar characteristics and have an equally significant impact on popular culture? How do these elements translate to a contemporary generation? In an era that mainstream society has often referred to as "Generation X," has there been any specific attention paid to the young disenfranchised Black male? Certainly these figures have made their mark in popular culture; it is now time that scholarly attention be paid to this group, which does more than simply reproduce sociological arguments that have long assumed a strident pathology. We must begin to ask ourselves, Why do these figures and the culture that they produce threaten so many people on one hand, and remain so popular with mass audiences on the other?

Has history made us become too accustomed to the tragic Black man, or will this image always be a part of American society? What are the historical precedents that define this figure? What are the cultural and class politics involved? These questions underlie this chapter and the scope of this book. In what ways have race, class, and gender come together to produce what are now regarded as "niggaz," "gangstaz,"

"G's," "O.G.'s," and "'hood rats"? What are they saying, and are they being heard? Are they simply a perceived threat, or are they real? Does their prominence as a monolithic representational form imply what the media consider to be appropriate images of African Americans, or does their representation in some way encompass what audiences want to see?

This chapter looks at three phases of contemporary Black male expression, paying specific attention to the way in which class has established clear boundaries between consecutive eras. In each case there are central figures who embody the sentiments of the era and suggest the possibilities for understanding and moving to the next phase. While none of these claims is scientific, I have pointed out several cultural icons, signposts, and events that help to define the era in question. Though there is a great deal of overlap, the three eras are still quite distinct.

First we will look at Bill Cosby, who represents the ideology of the race man. This is a bourgeois sentiment that locates its politics in the power of cultural advancement through what was once thought to be "uplifting the race." Cosby and his era embrace the assimilationist politics of Martin Luther King Jr. and see integration and a normalized Black upper class as representative of a politics of advancement. Positive representation, for both individuals and the race, as a way of critiquing years of negative representation, becomes paramount during this phase. This era roughly spans the duration of Cosby's successful television situation comedy (1984–92), especially through 1989, but begins to decline in influence during the late 1980s.

Secondly, Spike Lee represents the "New Black Aesthetic" (NBA) and uses the nationalist politics of Malcolm X to inform the era. Lee and other members of the NBA have grown up in the post–civil rights era and see individual power and access to the means of representation as significant goals. Though noble in their aspirations, the NBA and its bourgeois underpinnings can transcend the culture only in ways that bring individual success, but cannot address group elevation. Though the NBA offers cultural icons at an unprecedented level for African Americans, the surface value of this iconography cannot fully encompass the need for structural change. This phase can be said to have begun receiving public recognition with the release and ensuing controversy of Lee's *Do the Right Thing* in 1989. In many ways, it ended with the release and subsequent lack of controversy surrounding Lee's *Malcolm X* in 1992.

The third and final phase has no identifiable leader, nor does it embrace any overt form of politics; instead, this era is personified by several figures who possess similar characteristics and an open contempt for politics of any kind. The figure in question is the "nigga," and his politics are those of the "truly disadvantaged." Those who fall under this rubric have had the most impact on culture as well as the most destructive impact on themselves and their community. Their "don't give a fuck" attitude is compounded by the fact that so many outside of their communities subscribe to their messages. They occupy a world of chaos and nihilism that enriches at the same time that it destroys. The cultural impact of this strident duality forces all to pay attention, from the highest echelons of power to the lowest-level grassroots community leaders. They have affected our lives in a way that will never be forgotten.

Their presence also forces the agenda of class as an important consideration in attempting to define race in contemporary society. This era began receiving marginal attention with the release of NWA's *Straight outta Compton* in 1988, reached national recognition with the Los Angeles riots following the first Rodney King verdicts, and has currently evolved to the status of a societal threat as several conservative politicians have targeted the themes that it expresses as the fundamental threat to American morality.

The transition from the race man to the nigga personifies the most recent articulations of Black masculinity in popular culture. Key to each era are the class politics that distinguish one group from another. And as class politics have become more and more imperative in defining Blackness, we must look at the way these politics force us to reconsider race as an exclusive factor in understanding Black popular culture. Here the combination of race, class, and gender must be not only acknowledged, but ultimately dealt with critically as a way of advancing our understanding.

The Death of the Race Man

During the earlier part of the twentieth century and through the civil rights movement, the phrase "race man" was used in the Black community to refer to men who, through their efforts, exemplified excellence in the interest of, as Booker T. Washington had stated, "uplifting the race." The "race man" was a civil rights–era embodiment of what today falls under the highly contested term "role model." Cosby, and the proliferation of his image during the 1980s, fits perfectly with this model.

This tradition was defined by individuals who sought to provide representations that they hoped would reflect positively on the community. These figures were, according to Charles Henry, "to act as models of proper behavior for the black masses. Proper models hastened assimilation, while improper models flaunted independence" (37). A similarly problematic phrase, "a credit to the race," was often applied to boxer Joe Louis in the 1930s. These attempts to provide positive images were lauded in their time because of an underlying racist assumption that the African American race had no credit in the first place. Thus it was of the utmost importance that while working in the best interest of the race, one consistently work to nullify the negative stereotypes that plagued popular perception of the African American community. As Michelle Wallace has suggested, many of our society's gatekeepers assume that "the first job of Afro-American mass culture should be to uplift the race, or to salvage the denigrated image of blacks in the white American imagination" (*Invisibility Blues*, 1).

To some extent the aftermath of the civil rights era provided an opportunity for many to stray away from the rather strict tenets of race man ideology. Though race men were seen as promoters of the race at one time, subsequent generations would challenge this image and question its militancy. As time passed, singular attempts at affirming the paternalistic view of mainstream white society, or conservative Black society for that matter, were rejected. Instead, many African American males began openly challenging the codes of acceptable behavior and worked to defy all aspects of white society by establishing their own images of cool detachment and defiance.

The concept of the race man was applicable to African American cultural producers as well. Musicians, artists, and entertainers were celebrated or criticized for their ability to provide positive images, which inadvertently meant images that conformed to the acceptable standards of middle-class white behavior. The public figures who resisted this trend were equally reviled by assimilationist-minded individuals and embraced by those who sympathized with the emerging tenets of Black nationalist thought. Although jazz contains a good example of those who resisted these narrow configurations, such as the musicians of the bebop and post-bebop era, the full onset of defiant Black male images would begin in the 1960s, to become a permanent fixture in the ensuing decades.

The numerous Black male images in contemporary society expose us primarily to a new generation of performers who have come up after the rhetoric of the civil rights movement and the resulting political actions, which have not fully addressed the issue of societal racism. The previous decades offered some sense of an aspiration for racial equality that was supposedly inherent in the progression of time, yet was always delayed.

For instance, each of the world wars was thought of as a prime moment for the eradication of racism as a result of the increased awareness and exposure of it. Yet in both cases, with the site of activity being in either Europe or Asia and thus displaced from American soil, racial equality was never fully pursued after the wars. The civil rights movement was the last of these sites of struggle relative to racial equality, yet the ensuing generations have seen, minus the rhetoric of progress, that serious racial hierarchies as well as discrepancies in gender and class subordination define African American existence.

There have been no major social events in the last twenty-five years on the scale of a world war or a mass political movement such as the civil rights struggle. Vietnam functioned as a strident critique of progressive race rhetoric instead of affirming the good intentions of American political discourse after the conclusion of this highly contested war. Thus, the cultural producers who have come up in this modern era live in a world of disillusionment and cynicism, augmented by unparalleled access to the entertainment industry in the form of performers and in some cases executive positions that influence the production and exhibition of African American culture on a public scale. The civil rights movement did provide limited opportunities for individual African Americans in cultural production, yet it did little to change the lives of African Americans as a group. Individuals such as Bill Cosby and Oprah Winfrey command great power, capital, and respect in the industry, yet while their success is certainly progressive in one sense, their individual status is not enough to change the racism that has permeated this environment since its inception.

This text is concerned not with denied access to the means of representational production, but with a look at the currents that have emerged relative to a post–civil rights, post–Black Power generation of cultural producers and the forms of representation that result from their individual and collective efforts. Yet before the "new jacks" of the industry are addressed, it is important to analyze the transition from this older tradition of race-uplifting praxis to the contemporary generation, which has been acknowledged as providing a new Black aesthetic.

Am I Black Enough for Ya?: The Declining Significance of Cosby

At the conclusion of one of the most memorable episodes of *The Cosby Show*, we, as viewers, watch the Cosby family as they watch television file footage of Martin Luther King Jr.'s famous "I Have a Dream" speech. The speech by this time in American history had become so familiar that it needed no introduction. As the words echoed with the striking resonance of King's distinctive voice, individual family members stopped their activities and began to sit attentively in front of the television set. As spectators we were somehow induced into doing the same thing. Neither the words nor their implications needed an explanation.

This episode was broadcast in early 1986, the first year that Martin Luther King Jr.'s birthday was officially celebrated as a federal holiday. Like the image of King and the speech itself, Bill Cosby and *The Cosby Show* had become an accepted part of the American mainstream. It is as though King's rhetoric of assimilation, and the making of his birthday into a national holiday, had finally reached its pinnacle with the overwhelming success enjoyed by this upper-middle-class African American family of the 1980s.

With the racist history of American society as our background, we could now witness, based on the mass popularity of the show, that to some extent Cosby was being judged on the content of his televisual character instead of merely on the color of his skin. This entrance into the corridors of capitalism, commodity culture, and the representation of mainstream television meant that Cosby was, in this truly American construction, "free at last." His link with the ultimate icon of acceptance and assimilation, Martin Luther King Jr., was a strong endorsement of this move to the mainstream. For all intents and purposes, the image of Bill Cosby, particularly as presented on *The Cosby Show*, was the last of race man imagery.

Using the metaphor of King and the civil rights movement to inform the program's political sentiment, we can see that Cosby's concern was with projecting images that foregrounded the most positive attributes of the race, while ignoring a discussion of race and racism. Herman Gray sets forth the context of African Americans on television that *The Cosby Show* exhibited: "in television representations of blacks, the historical realities of slavery, discrimination, and racism or the persistent struggles against domination are displaced and translated into celebrations of black middle class visibility and achievement" (378). Cosby's presentation aimed to establish a solidly upper-class existence which, though it did focus to some extent on race, came across to many as being applicable on a universal scale and thus was not racially specific enough regarding the plight of African Americans.

This idea of mass applicability was often viewed as being problematic on the question of Blackness, because of the program's failure to directly confront racial and economic issues. Also, the program flourished against the backdrop of Reagan-era politics, which not only emphasized capitalist excess but led to the popular image of the conservative Black ideologue, such as Clarence Pendleton, Thomas Sowell, and eventually Clarence Thomas.

Herman Gray linked the program's success and massive popular appeal to this conservative mentality that circulated during this period and in turn derided what he saw as the assimilationist objective of *The Cosby Show*. Gray states in discussing the cultural context in which Cosby was successful that "the primacy of individual effort over collective possibilities, the centrality of individual values, morality, and initiative, and a benign (if not invisible) social structure are the key social terms that define television discourses about black success and failure" (397). Similar to Gray, Michelle Wallace critiques the program on the basis of its reduction of cultural difference to commodity status: "culture is then reduced to a style of consumption that offers up, say, expensive exotic-looking handknit sweaters, or a brief scene of the Cosbys at a jazz club where a black woman is singing rather than any concrete or complex textualization of cultural difference" (2).

In both Gray's and Wallace's construction, the prevalence of a bourgeois sentiment, either in society as a whole or specifically on the show, is regarded as denying the articulation of race. Not only are the issues of race and upper-class existence seen as incompatible, but Cosby's embrace of the bourgeois life in essence nullifies creation aspects of his Blackness. Herman Gray states that *Cosby* is "just Black enough not to offend and middle class enough to comfort" (122).

While I am sympathetic to both Gray's and Wallace's argument, as they have engaged commodity culture and its pitfalls for cultural identity quite well, their notions of race and class assume that there is a correct formula for Black identity that should in some way address working-class politics. Inherent in this notion is the assumption that Blackness is indelibly linked to a working-class ethos and singularly informed by the struggles of overcoming poverty. Thus those who do not embrace this notion of Blackness are seen as selling out or—the ultimate charge—of not being Black enough.

In response to the argument that a tension exists between race, class, and cultural identity relative to Cosby, Michael Dyson suggests that "it is certainly healthy for Cosby not to be obsessed with race consciousness, which would indicate that black life is lived only in response to white racism, that black culture is merely reactive and is incapable of forming visions of life beyond the reach of race" (*Reflecting Black*, 83).[1]

Yet my concern here is not whether Cosby was properly Black; instead, I am interested in using Cosby as a metaphor for a past era. While there is merit to all of these critical responses to this most popular public icon, the bottom line for me has to do with media access, cultural representation, and the death of a popular form. Cosby assumed a great deal of importance throughout the 1980s, almost to the point of denying any other form of popular African American imagery. As far as mainstream culture is concerned, it is as though the representation of African American culture operates only monolithically, and that only one form of popular representation may be available at any given time.

African American life is not monolithic, so it should be represented broadly so as to accommodate its broad dimensions. Representations of whiteness seem to always span the spectrum of good and evil, high and low. For every episode of *Dallas* or *Dynasty*, which display the grotesque wealth of the upper class, there are counterparts in programs such as *Roseanne* which focus on the travails of working-class life. In addition, numerous other programs push neither extreme of the class issue and instead present whiteness and middle-class status as being normalized within the context of mainstream America.

Our aim as critics should be focused on media institutions that deny a more informed representation of African American culture. We must accept that as we proceed into the next century, the reconfiguration of Black identity will be informed by a myriad of possibilities, including gender, class, and sexuality. As these concerns become more prominent in both public and private discussions of African American identity, we will be forced to realize that the complexities of cultural identity are too difficult to be reduced to the redundant question of being "Black enough." And as we take into consideration the impact that these questions will have, it becomes apparent that the trope of the race man and his resulting ideology will be too limiting for the full understanding of an empowered African American culture.

The political impact of Cosby's representation was similar to that of the civil rights movement, specifically a post–civil rights approach to the question of race. Cosby represents an assimilated world where the persistent issues of race and upper-class existence for African Americans have been normalized. These issues are no longer in need of discussion as they have been transformed into more universal, thus humanistic, causes, what many would consider race-transcending. Dyson argues that "Cosby presents a black universe as the norm, feeling no need to announce the imposition of African- American perspectives, since they are assumed" (87). Race, in this example, has been assimilated into the fabric of American society; thus the older middle-class Black politics of the era has been addressed fully and is no longer in need of the overt attention once accorded it.

Cosby's presence and eventual retirement from the program after eight amazingly successful years demonstrate the death of the race man and the birth of a new Black aesthetic. The end of this era proved that the limitations of positive representation had never been fully realized. Cosby clearly provided what people had requested in the form of a positive representation, but his appearance failed to address the historical racism and continued denial of African American presence and control over the means of visual production relative to popular culture.

Although Cosby (and others) prospered individually during this time, racism in the media and in society was still operating at very high levels. Certainly Cosby made his impact, but it was now obvious that positive images alone were not bringing about any structural change. Ironically, the broadcast of Cosby's last episode coincided with the first night of the Los Angeles riots of April 1992 in the aftermath of the Rodney King verdicts. If ever there was an appropriate gesture to mark the end of the rather passive reign of Cosby—which had declined in influence substantially by the end—it was the situation in the volatile streets of Los Angeles.

Spike Lee and the New Black Aesthetic

As the streets of Los Angeles went up in flames, it became apparent that a renewed sense of urgency had taken hold in the urban environment. This same sense of urgency had begun to inform much of African American culture as well. The extensive video footage of the riots clearly suggests that the events were less about political effort than about self-aggrandizement and material possessions. This lower-class version of laissez-faire capitalism made public a newly emergent image and recurrent mentality, in clear opposition to that of the race man, which was now informing the postindustrial urban landscape.

With the absence of Cosby, the death of the race man, and the declining significance of both the civil rights agenda as an influential social movement and Martin Luther King Jr. as an icon of popular culture of the 1980s, we witnessed the rise of a new generation of African American cultural producers. This new wave is loosely composed of African Americans who came of age after the civil rights and Black Power eras, whose initial recognition of African American culture resulted from the images that proliferated during the 1970s, and whose ambivalent relationship to the previously constraining dictates of both mainstream and African American culture informs their work.

This generational shift clearly establishes the boundaries between the older image represented by Cosby and the "new jacks" of African American cultural production. According to Houston Baker, a generational shift is "an ideologically motivated movement overseen by young or newly emergent intellectuals dedicated to refuting the work of their intellectual predecessors and to establishing a new framework for intellectual inquiry" (*Blues, Ideology,* 67). While Baker locates the shift in intellectual terms, I use this idea as it applies to popular culture.

In this regard, the new generation of African American cultural producers and their work fit in somewhere with the phrase coined by novelist Trey Ellis, the "New Black Aesthetic" (NBA). Ellis, author of *Platitudes* (1988) and *Home Repairs* (1993), suggests that there is at work an "open-ended New Black Aesthetic" inherited from "a few Seventies pioneers that shamelessly borrows and reassembles across both race and class lines" ("New Black Aesthetic," 20). Clearly, class becomes the key issue.

Those who make up this new generation have grown up in an era in which overt racial discrimination in the form of Jim Crow laws or separate facilities has been outlawed, allowing access to the corridors of middle-class society on an individual basis. Therefore the opportunity to attend elite universities and to be associated with the best of our society's corporate conglomerate media institutions is not so much the exception anymore. As was quite noticeable during the Clarence Thomas confirmation hearings, a number of African Americans have attended Ivy League schools. Ellis sees the opening up of the educational process as significant to the proliferation of the NBA. He defines a cultural "mulatto" as one who is "educated by a multi-racial mix of cultures" and can "navigate easily in the white world."

Spike Lee is a perfect example of this new generation, having attended Morehouse, the citadel of the Black male bourgeois, and the highly regarded New York University film school. The fact that Lee often sells the racial wolf tickets of Black nationalism is somewhat less threatening when we consider that his films now command the attention befitting a true Hollywood *auteur*, and that he is one of the few African Americans in Hollywood who can regularly count on their projects' being given the coveted "green light." The fact that Warner Brothers and Universal are featured on his resumé increases the viability of his mulatto status.

Lee represents the transition point between the two eras. Greg Tate sees Lee's artistic and commercial success as a significant progression over previous generations of cultural producers. Tate suggests that Lee is to be praised for overloading his "joint with black in-jokes and semiotic codes," but also for pushing "an uncompromisingly black vision to blacks through mainstream distribution, exhibition, and media channels" (208).

The key point of emphasis in both Ellis's and Tate's analyses of this new era is the ability of Black cultural producers to infiltrate mainstream white institutions while still providing some sense of an African American aesthetic. Ultimately, the commodity status of Blackness becomes integral in distinguishing this marketability now associated with foregrounding the question of race. This is clearly different from Cosby's attempts to provide positive images which minimized any outward demonstration of one's cultural identity and at the same time had mainstream appeal. With the new generation, one could be as Black as one wanted and still occupy a significant position in the marketplace of culture.

Yet this discussion of a new Black aesthetic clearly entails a middle-class notion of Blackness that uses these tropes as a way of attaining a heightened sense of individual autonomy. When cultural identity becomes a marketable commodity which is easily manipulated, it ultimately loses its impact on culture. Spike Lee is certainly considered less of a threatening phenomenon to the mainstream now than when he first burst onto the cultural scene.

This era, as well as the situation itself, finds its central figure in the image of Malcolm X, and Lee's film *Malcolm X* assists in establishing the cultural dilemma confronting this new generation. Lee's public campaign to gain control of the film, his arguments with several other African Americans, most notably Amiri Bakara, over his ability to properly render the life of Malcolm X in film, and his financial difficulties in completing the project were the events that defined this highly contested moment surrounding the release of what is arguably the most important Black film to date. Yet soon after its release, the conversation stopped. Lee was no longer the media darling; nor was Malcolm X's image the point of serious contention that it had been. The reason is that both Lee and the film had demonstrated that there was nothing to be concerned about. Both the film and the filmmaker were now seen in their true light, that of middle-class acceptability.

The film's opening scene demonstrates this point. Having been subjected to several months of publicity about the filmmaker's struggle in getting the film made and having this discourse situate the viewer, we witness the redundant image of the Rodney King beating, which slowly dissolves into a burning *X* now visibly displaying the American flag. We are presented with Lee's objective from the outset: placing Malcolm X in the pantheon of important *American* political figures. Immediately following this graphic opening scene, we witness a close-up shot of Spike Lee himself, which is later revealed to be his character of Shorty, Malcolm's friend.

The fact that the first fictional image we see is that of Lee, which we have seen repeatedly prior to the film itself, suggests that the image of

Malcolm is subordinate to Lee's image, thus positing the filmmaker's own sense of importance. It is as though Lee's struggle to get the film produced is equated with, if not made superior to, Malcolm's own political struggles in life. Through this self-serving cinematic transformation, Spike Lee and the image of Malcolm X become problematically interchangeable. This is implied even further by the linking of personal and political in the title of Lee's book on the making of the film, which discusses "by any means necessary: the trials and tribulations of making a film while ten million motherfuckers are fucking with you."

Even at the film's conclusion, when we see and hear several Black children boldly declaring, "I am Malcolm X," it seems apparent that the filmmaker's own sense of cultural importance is really what is being displaced, but unequivocally enunciated, that he himself is being put forward as a modern-day version of Malcolm X. The use of Malcolm X as an example of contemporary Black masculinity has become quite popular; witness Joe Woods's revealingly titled collection of essays *Malcolm X: In Our Own Image*, Nathan McCall's *Make Me Wanna Holler*, or Michael Dyson's *Making Malcolm*, in which he combines personal experience with critical discourse to demonstrate Malcolm's lasting significance in many of our lives. This is obviously the road that Lee is pursuing as well, but while Wood, McCall, and Dyson use Malcolm's life as metaphor, Lee uses a purported historical examination as autobiography.

Lee also repeatedly equated himself publicly with filmmaker Oliver Stone during the discourse preceding the film, further demonstration of his use of the image of Malcolm X to highlight the struggle of a Black man to be accepted as equal to white men such as Stone in the eyes of Hollywood. While this is an admirable political attempt on Lee's part to expose the blatant inequality of Hollywood, one must question the prostitution of Malcolm's image to achieve it. Though Lee's presence in Hollywood has undoubtedly benefited other African American filmmakers, this gesture of inappropriate and ahistorical self-importance obscures an otherwise significant point.

Lee's highly publicized financial donations from several prominent African American celebrities seemed to strengthen the film's importance as a cultural object, but the publicity also minimized the historical and political significance of the much-anticipated text. As the rather lengthy closing credit sequence ambles along, we see several of these celebrities wearing Lee's trademark *X* baseball caps. Among them is Bill Cosby, which suggests that the race man and the neo–Black nationalist position have somehow merged as the result of a similarity in economic and cultural capital. This seems less a demonstration of gratitude and more a celebration of Lee's elite circle of friends, clearly inappropriate in a film of such historical and political magnitude.

It would not be too farfetched to suggest that Malcolm's political struggles have made possible the rise of a Black celebrity class whose wealth we can all admire but never truly take part in. It is as though the birth of a contemporary class of African American celebrities is the fulfillment of all the aspirations articulated in Malcolm's teachings, that the African American celebrity is equivalent to or a substitute for a truly liberated race of people.

In the end, there is no doubt that Lee's mainstreaming of himself and the image of Malcolm X is still considered part of a Black aesthetic, one that is acknowledged by both Ellis and Tate, but what is truly novel is that these images are equally Black and bourgeois. Using this situation as a strong example of contemporary cultural identity and its commodity status reveals the middle-class foundation of the new Black aesthetic and the increasing regularity with which it has infiltrated the mainstream, as opposed to threatening it.

The difference here has to do with what infiltrating the mainstream could be argued to have done for the cultural figures in question. The idea of selling out—clearly still an issue during Cosby's era, and certainly in the era following as well—seems to be defined differently in the case of Spike Lee and the new Black aesthetic. Lee's rhetoric of Black nationalism, though it functions as a venue for personal gain, is political enough on the surface that claims about compromising one's ideological position would appear to be inappropriate. We must acknowledge Lee's laudable efforts as a pioneering figure in the resurgence of Black cinema. His 40 Acres and a Mule film studio and his merchandising efforts and marketing schemes have undoubtedly contributed to the lasting impact of African American popular culture. With this in mind, his claims of forwarding a politicized Black aesthetic quell all questions of compromise and bring us to the point of his infiltration when we recognize that his multiple associations with several corporate and media entities afford him significant individual viability in contemporary culture.

In contemporary society, not only does one look to a redefined form of Black nationalism to gain a sense of space relative to the mainstream, but, considering that any group access to the mainstream may be as difficult, individual access to and accumulation of capital have come to take the place of group enfranchisement. I am not condemning the new Black aesthetic for its infiltration of the mainstream; as a matter of fact,

I would celebrate many of the resulting gains. I am simply recognizing the limitations of this process for Black popular culture.

Although the older philosophies of the race man had become outdated by the time of the new Black aesthetic, the new era builds on the bourgeois underpinning of the previous movement. Yet the NBA can be extended to accommodate the rhetoric of a self-righteous Black nationalism that in turn set the tone for the challenge to come as the NBA slowly became entrenched in the mainstream.

Over time, Spike Lee's importance as a filmmaker would decline as his significance as a popular icon increased. The cult of celebrity now placed Lee firmly in its center. The memorable image of Lee's courtside exchange with Reggie Miller during the 1994 National Basketball Association Eastern Conference Finals at Madison Square Garden signified Lee's celebrity status as equal to that of Jack Nicholson, a familiar courtside presence at Lakers games during the 1980s. Lee and his generation of cultural producers have been transformed into mainstream icons whose politics may have remained intact, but whose influence as the avant-garde of black popular culture may have given way to a more insurgent cultural impulse.

Other members of what was once called the new Black aesthetic have also become entrenched in mainstream institutions. The now-defunct rap group Public Enemy, once regarded as militant, began opening for the popular rock group U2, while Wynton and Branford Marsalis separately infiltrated two of the most traditional mainstream institutions, albeit with lingering controversy, through their association with New York's Lincoln Center and the *Tonight Show*, respectively. Once again, what was previously seen as selling out becomes a positive progression for Black popular culture. The mainstream is constantly transformed by those who infiltrate it and who become more influential at a corporate level, but less significant from the perspective of cultural impact on Black popular audiences, especially for those who make up the lower class.

It is interesting how one audience can perceive this move to the mainstream as becoming part of the establishment, while another sees it as a threat toward losing power. Thus it is not uncommon to find individuals who are criticized by mainstream audiences as being "too Black," or at least pushing a Black agenda, and at the same time are criticized by another Black audience as having sold out.

In presiding over the prestigious Jazz at Lincoln Center program, Wynton Marsalis is the first African American to sit in any seat of power relative to what is arguably the most prestigious cultural venue in the country. Over the last few years, Marsalis has been accused by many white jazz critics, including author Gene Les in his controversial book *Cats of Many Colors*—which suggests that these practices amount to a reverse racism—of excluding white musicians and their works from the program. On the other hand, Marsalis is often criticized by African Americans for his conservative embrace of tradition at the expense of new forms of jazz expression, especially the avant-garde. His vociferous critiques of rap music and other forms of contemporary Black expression, especially lower-class expressions, are consistent with the most conservative mainstream political voices. It is clear that his vision of jazz, which seems to revolve around reestablishing Duke Ellington's vast musical canon, is threatening to the white jazz establishment, who have historically overemphasized the contributions of white jazz musicians to the idiom, but have always had the majority of the public space in which to express their opinions. Yet Marsalis's link, both personally and philosophically, with conservative African American writers Albert Murray and Stanley Crouch, along with his limited view of contemporary Black culture, is equally problematic for an entirely different audience.

The oscillation in audience perceptions regarding race and class is a regular occurrence, as many of the newly found positions of power by African Americans raise questions that one never considered one would have to ask. This is indeed a class issue, as middle- and upper-class accessibility through culture engenders numerous contradictions regarding questions that were once thought to be exclusive to race. For this reason, our attention shifts from the new Black aesthetic to the evolution of the most recent form of popular Black culture, the emergence of what I will refer to as the nigga, where the lines of delineation are less confusing but no less complex.

Niggaz 4 Life

The concept of the nigga is a return to an older form of Black masculinity in popular culture, but rejuvenated relative to the circumstances of contemporary culture. One of the most contested terms in the history of the English language is the racial designation "nigger." At the highest level the term connotes the racial hierarchy that has defined America since its inception. Specifically demarcating the abiding rule of white society from the ultimate social inferiority linked with African Americans, "nigger" remains a lingering example of the culture defined by slavery and the world that grew up in its aftermath.

Though "African American" may be the contemporary name most readily accepted as the proper term of identification, there have been several monikers applied throughout American history which have over time become obsolete. Terms such as "colored," "Negro," and most recently "Black," have been deemed unacceptable to many as inconsistent with the changes in society. And though there are still people who identify themselves as "colored" (the National Association for the Advancement of Colored People), or "Negro" (the United Negro College Fund), and a large segment of society who still use "Black" as the ultimate signifier, none of these terms has the consistent power of the denigration implied through the use of "nigger." Though it is considered improper in formal public conversation, it is obvious that the word still has a great deal of currency in much of the private sector, and increasingly in the public sector as well. For example, one of the highlights of the pre-trial hearings in the O.J. Simpson case was a heated exchange between two African American attorneys about the historical significance of the word "nigger."

In suggesting that the use of the term by the defense would bias African American jurors, Christopher Darden, attorney for the prosecution, described it as the "filthiest, nastiest, dirtiest word in the English language." Celebrity attorney for the defense Johnnie Cochran countered by suggesting that "African Americans live with offensive words, offensive looks, and offensive treatment every day of their lives, but they still believe in this country." This exchange illustrated the contention associated with this word and made the normally private debate (though it has had its own history in the African American community for some time) public for a mass audience.

This public court debate is just one example of the contentiousness surrounding this word and, more important, the image that it conjures up.[2] Yet what is truly compelling about this word and its resulting image is that many in contemporary society, in opposition to a large percentage of African Americans, have chosen to adopt a nuanced form of the word as a vital part of their own cultural identity. The modern-day "nigga," having come to prominence through several cultural arenas including rap music, African American cinema, and professional sports, equally defies aspects of mainstream white culture, as well as the at times restrictive dimensions of status quo Black culture.

Ultimately the defining characteristic of the modern-day nigga is class, as opposed to what used to be exclusively race. According to historian Robin Kelly, the nigga is "a product of the ghetto." Kelly goes on to say that niggaz link "their identity to the hood instead of simply skin color" and that the use of the term acknowledges "the limitations of racial politics, including black middle-class reformism as well as black nationalism" (210). As Kelly points out, the fact that this metaphor has been recurrently embraced suggests the importance that the issue of class holds in relation to contemporary definitions of cultural identity.

What is interesting here, though, is that the issue of class begins to take on significant dimensions relative to contemporary culture. Because of the residual effects of the opening of the marketplace in the post–civil rights era on an individual basis, many African American entertainers have been afforded an opportunity to make large sums of money, thus creating an elite class of entertainers. As access to capital indicates some sense of freedom in capitalist America, several of these benefactors have been given the opportunity to live in bourgeois comfort while presenting an image that references the lower-class specifics of the nigga mentality. It is not uncommon to find individuals who can oscillate between the two poles.

A good example can also be found in the public presentation of O.J. Simpson. On the surface, Simpson was successful in projecting a public image of race- and class-transcending mainstream appeal, yet the tone of the 911 audio tape recorded during one of his spousal-abuse episodes reveals the underlying components of aggressive rage and violent assertion that often have been associated with the extremes of Black masculinity. In other words, the desire for access to capital forced Simpson into a position that would momentarily transcend race and class for the purposes of public imagery, yet the privacy of intimate relations seemingly allowed a much more race- and class-distinct response. For the purposes of money and success, specific definitions of race and class were made secondary to a more acceptable mainstream image that worked to obscure the extremes of these definitions.

Yet this type of duality is less prevalent in today's society than the open flaunting of the nigga persona. Access to capital has made it possible for many to defy the accepted codes of mainstream decorum in favor of displaying a defiant mode of aggression whenever desired, as long as they can continue to be profitable from an industry perspective. Because the accumulation of extensive capital has allowed for a more open display of race- and class-distinct imagery, questions arise as to whether the race man ideology has become unpopular. Yes, the race man has become extinct in a cultural arena where positive images seem less imperative in winning the adulation of large segments of the African American community as well as mainstream society. As a matter of fact, the visibility of the nigga has opened up the dialogue on imagery from a class perspective that seldom gets addressed in public.

Whereas Cosby was often referred to as a "role model," basketball player Charles Barkley, a good example of a figure who embodies the characteristics of the nigga, declares in a highly controversial Nike commercial,

> I am not a role model. I am not paid to be a role model.
> I am paid to wreak havoc on a basketball court.
> Parents should be role models. Just because I can dunk
> a basketball doesn't mean I should raise your kids.

Barkley's comments, though valid in one sense, make clear his refusal to accept the race man ideology or the politically progressive ideology of the new Black aesthetic.

This is confounded even further by Barkley's many public remarks about the amount of money he makes and the freedom associated with the possession of that money. A comment that he made in 1992, that he was a "'90s nigga" who could do what he wanted, signified the liberated notion traditionally associated with rich white males that Barkley, as a consequence of his own financial status, could now claim as well, but in a specifically Black way.

The emphasis on the nigga has to do with this mentality as it is articulated through popular culture. Whereas Cosby's generation personified the socially erect race man, and the new Black aesthetic and its focus on bourgeois nationalism dealt with the politics of race and infiltration of the mainstream, the most recent generation defies both the decorum of social acceptability and the overtly political nature of the new Black aesthetic.

Both of the earlier movements looked to gain access to the mainstream in one way or another. The nigga is not interested in anything having to do with the mainstream, though his cultural products are clearly an integral part of mainstream popular culture. The nigga rejects the mainstream even though he has already been absorbed by it.

On the other hand, the nigga, interested in maintaining status in the world of alternative capital, may take on many of the tenets of mainstream society, but take them to the level of excess. Educational background influenced the progression of the two earlier movements. The nigga, in contrast, not only is uneducated, but sees value only in being educated in the ways of the streets and the hard-core urban environment that he exists in.

Those who fall into this category are most accurately defined by William Julius Wilson as "the truly disadvantaged." Wilson suggests that there is a viable underclass of African Americans who are in a sense beyond the reach of communal or government intervention. These individuals are the most extreme victims of the changes in the American urban landscape in the post industrial era. Wilson argues that "urban minorities have been particularly vulnerable to structural economic changes, such as the shift from goods-producing to service-producing industries, the increasing polarization of the labor market into low-wage and high-wage sectors, technological innovations, and the relocation of manufacturing industries out of the central cities" (39).

The truly disadvantaged represent the failure of social policy in addressing the needs not only of race but, more important, also of class as it pertains to a contemporary notion of Blackness. Wilson expounds on the characteristics of this group, who "lack training and skills and either experience long-term unemployment or are not members of the labor force, individuals who are engaged in street crime and other forms of aberrant behavior, and families that experience long- term spells of poverty and/or welfare dependency" (8). He adds that the dimensions of this underclass are so specific that they "depict a reality not captured in the more standard designation lower class." Consequently the underclass, because of its specific circumstances, also begins to assume a certain lifestyle and a certain mentality based on these distinct social conditions.

Key in this social experience, certainly as far as popular culture is concerned, is the reliance on the underworld economy of drug dealing, the near-infinitesimal chance of playing professional sports, especially basketball, or the pursuit of a career in the music industry, most notably the rap world. Rapper Biggie Smalls spells it out perfectly: "If I wasn't in the rap game / I'd probably have a key knee in the crack game / Ya see, the streets is a short stop / Either you slingin' crack rock or you got a wicked jump shot."

The venue of rap serves as a means of upward mobility and social legitimation, allowing Biggie Smalls to describe the dismal choices faced by those who attempt to rise up out of the ghetto. Playing professional basketball, a slim possibility at best, is often desired but seldom realized, while participation in the drug trade seems to require little more than the willingness to make money and, if necessary, die in the line of duty. Thus basketball and rap become the primary vehicles for the articulation of an underclass aesthetic here associated with the nigga.

Rap is obviously an extension of the Black oral tradition and the legacy of Black music and its relationship to the cultural landscape of America. Gangsta rap, with its origins on the West Coast, specifically addresses the worldview of the truly disadvantaged. In understanding this cultural form, it is important to recognize the historical context from which it emerges.

Folk culture is the essence of any cultural articulation. As far as African American culture in the twentieth century is concerned, folk culture can be defined as the blues. And while the blues may be one of the most misunderstood forms in American culture, the "meaning of the blues," as I have described elsewhere, involves the range of emotions that African American life may include.[3] All of the most significant forms of African American articulation in this century have been developed from the blues idiom. The blues entails more than just a depressed state of mind; it encompasses high and low and everything in between.

A good example of the working of the blues in contemporary society can be found in Ice Cube's poignant "It Was a Good Day." The song represents the full range of life possibilities for the truly disadvantaged urban Black male. The tune is an effective, though ironic, commentary on daily life in the 'hood. What would normally be considered mundane aspects of life are transformed into celebratory aspects of surviving another day. Ice Cube concludes by stating, "Today I didn't even have to use my AK / I gotta say it was a good day."

In this sense rap is the perfect continuation of an oral tradition, but in a way specific to contemporary society. It is one of the few avenues for the articulation of lower-class black male angst relative to the post-industrial environment. Basketball is another. Much as the primary tool for rapping is a voice and the ability to flow lyrically, basketball requires few materials: a ball, which someone in the community will certainly have, and a basket, which will often be located in a park or other public place to which those in the community have access. In other words, the truly disadvantaged, though possessing little in the way of material goods, need only the opportunity to transform space into a viable form of African American expression. And though rap and basketball function quite well in this way, it is the extension of this phenomenon into the realm of visual culture that allows for the significance of African American film and the prominence of music videos to define the present moment.

It is the transfer of the blues impulse, and its contemporary embodiment, rap, to cinema, television, and video that creates our most illuminating examples of cultural commentary in contemporary society. The fact that many of these instances are the product of the truly disadvantaged Black male perspective, in a world where Black women tend to dominate the "high" cultural realm of literature and fiction (e.g., Toni Morrison, Alice Walker, Terry McMillan), suggests that the intricacies of race, class, and gender are often brought together across the metaphorical body of the African American male. It is not coincidental that this body is closely associated in the public imagination with either sex or death.

The cases of Clarence Thomas, Mike Tyson, Tupac Shakur, Snoop Doggy Dogg, and O.J. Simpson have each suggested, in one way or another, that the granting of power in one sense, be it economic, cultural, or political, must be augmented by the abuse of power in another sense. In other words, Black men with power, and their assumed hypersexuality and ultraviolent nature, are the ultimate societal threat.

The most persistent threat of Black masculinity has been murderous and sexual in nature, as *Birth of a Nation*, the cornerstone of twentieth-century American film culture, demonstrates so vividly. Thus the public integration of these issues and their almost exclusive association with the truly disadvantaged Black male in contemporary society should come as no surprise. Even the questionable circumstances of race, gender, and sexuality that surround pop superstar Michael Jackson begin in the industrial confines of Gary, Indiana, and reach an apex with public accusations of child molestation, an abuse of power via sex in a totally different, but ultimately similar sense.

In each of these examples we can find the denial of power in someone's class background, which seems to ultimately result in the abuse of power once that person has gained a significant financial and cultural position. Yet in each case it is the mentality of the truly disadvantaged that was formulated in these individuals' childhood and the continued embrace of this mentality long after these circumstances have faded from their lives that problematizes their existence. And when these tensions are articulated in public, they tend to be expressed in the same way.

Although on the surface there appear to be substantial differences between Clarence Thomas and Snoop, there really is little difference when you consider that the celebration of sexual prowess emerges from the same truly disadvantaged place, and what is really troubling to the rest of society is the fact that these reprehensible thoughts are now allowed mainstream presentation. In other words, the truly disadvantaged are fine as long as they stay in their truly disadvantaged place, unless like Thomas they eliminate their former association with this background by attempting to eradicate this "underclass" through public policy.

This also shows that though many consider the truly disadvantaged threatening, there are still those opportunists among us who see the value of their talents, be it conservative Republicans or greedy music industry executives. It is the truly disadvantaged as a perspective and cultural ethos that provides America with both some of its most threatening imagery and some its most profitable commodities. The cultural combination of a disenfranchised race and a disempowered class emerges as critical and cathartic at the same time. In a contemporary American society where trigger-happy, nuclear-minded Communists are no longer a perceived threat and bomb-toting Islamic fundamentalists are too far removed from the daily lives of most Americans, the homegrown threat of the truly disadvantaged Black male remains prominent. The potential entrance of this threatening figure into mainstream society, be it on the Supreme Court or on the best-selling record charts, while providing economic rewards for some who are already in power, can be the ultimate mechanism of fear when used as a weapon of diversion for the rest of society.

It is for this reason that public outcries such as those articulated as conservative sentiment against affirmative action—the one remote possibility for most of the truly disadvantaged to enter the professional arena—are being castigated for denying white male privilege. In the meantime, the real threat to the flimsy fabric that now holds America together, the truly disadvantaged white male, sets his sights on a government which he sees as failing him and in return bombs a federal building as an overt expression of his anger. In a country where the right hand truly does not know what the left hand is doing, the subterfuge of race provided an opportunity for the often ignored, but truly dangerous, appearance of race and class in a form that America has used to its own advantage but seldom acknowledged as a serious threat to its own continued existence. Thus the truly disadvantaged Black male is once again relegated to the status of perceived threat, while the real threat lies in the perverted mentality that assumes a Black privilege but resonates with a white lower-class denial of power. Race becomes a scapegoat, while class becomes the prevailing issue. The continued articulation of class in a number of forms specific to Black masculinity defines the focus of the following chapters. The expression of these sentiments through popular culture defines some of the most significant societal commentary on present conditions.

Check Yo Self Before You Wreck Yo Self: The Death of Politics in Rap Music and Popular Culture

Rap music is the most visible form of African American cultural expression in contemporary society. With its emergence we have also seen a change in African American popular culture specific to the late 1980s and early 1990s. The recent proliferation of African American film and televisual representation, with rap music serving as a primary means of influence, has led to new definitions of contemporary African American popular culture in both the academic and the public domain.[1]

One of the most interesting discussions has involved the thematic resurgence of a politically charged voice that these forms provide a perfect venue for expressing. The rise and eventual fall of this political discourse in popular culture is closely tied to the public presentation of popular forms. In its political dimensions, popular culture, having reached an apex with the release of Public Enemy's second album, *It Takes a Nation of Millions to Hold Us Back* (1988), seems to have functioned as a genre whose popularity had passed, instead of a sustained movement which connected both cultural artifacts and "real" political events, as did similar movements in the late 1960s and early 1970s.[2]

The emergence of gangsta rap has seen an open rejection of politics by those involved. Publicly echoed in Dr. Dre's ever-popular "Dre Day" we hear a complete disregard for "medallions, dreadlocks, and black fists," obvious markers for the more political aspirations of those interested in Black nationalism or what is now commonly called "Afrocentricity." This rejection of a political agenda is consistent with Spike Lee's mainstreaming of the most important figure of Black nationalism, Malcolm X, in the 1992 film by that title. These events mark the end of a political flirtation in rap music and, by extension, African American popular culture.

An interesting case study that examines the highs and lows of political discourse in rap music—similar to what Cornel West calls the "new cultural politics"—and the gradual displacement of this agenda by gangsta rap can be found in the meteoric rise of 1993's Grammy Award–winning best new act, Arrested Development. Using images of a critical spirituality, southern existence, stylized forms of dress, and an overall ideology of Afrocentrism, Arrested Development engaged an empowered critique of both external racism and the internal neglect that set them apart from other rap acts in the early 1990s. This political stance endeared them to many as the embodiment of a progressive discourse surrounding culture, society, and politics.

Rap and The "New Cultural Politics of Difference"

Rap can be used to analyze the mutually illuminating yet divergent categories of race, class, and gender in African American society. More often than not, questions of race dominate both popular and critical discussions about rap music. Though this discussion is undoubtedly important, contemporary society, especially in the post–Reagan/Bush era, forces us to deal with the influence of the class struggle on African American society.

At the same time, an empowered female voice that fuses the issues of race, class, and gender would also open up possibilities for understanding the nuances of contemporary African American culture. As Tricia Rose points out, "through their lyrics and video images, black women rappers form a dialogue with working class black women and men, offering young black women a small but potent culturally-reflexive public space" ("Never Trust," 114). Though this female voice in rap has gained significant momentum over the last few years, there remains much to be desired, both artistically and in terms of intellectual response.[3]

The cultural and economic base of this music emphasizes the African presence in American society, which makes the foregrounding of race and class struggle paramount in understanding this cultural practice. Certain elements of rap music seem to have the potential to exemplify what Cornel West has labeled the "new cultural politics of difference."

> **The new cultural politics of difference are neither simply opposi-
> tional in contesting the mainstream for inclusion, nor transgressive in
> the avant-gardist sense of shocking conventional bourgeois audi-
> ences. Rather, they are distinct articulations of talented contributors
> to culture who desire to align themselves with demoralized, demobi-
> lized, depoliticized and disorganized people in order to empower
> and enable social action and, if possible, to enlist collective insur-
> gency for the expansion of freedom, democracy, and individuality.**
>
> ("The New Politics," 19–20)

African American culture is replete with examples of this new cultural politics of difference, particularly in regard to the influence of lower-class politics in understanding race. In many respects, by the late 1980s and the early 1990s, the presentation of anything as an "authentic" reflection of African American culture had to revolve in some way around the exploits and endeavors of the lumpenproletariat. It was necessary in this construction for race and class to consistently inform one another.

The most overt demonstration of this desire for cultural "authenticity" was white rapper Vanilla Ice's claim that he grew up in the midst of African American poverty and was once a victim of gang violence. He was identifying with Blackness based not on his race but on the extent of his association with lower-class African American existence. In other words, his class status made him "Black."

Along the same lines, the all-white rap group Young Black Teenagers claim that Blackness is a "state of mind"—undoubtedly a ghetto mindset. The impetus for forming the rock band in the film *The Commitments* (1991) serves as another example. According to the film's main character, the group members can identify with African American music because of their multiple oppression as Northern Irish working-class Catholics. "The Irish are the Blacks of Europe, and the Dubliners are the Blacks of Ireland, and the Northsiders are the Blacks of Dublin. So say it loud, I'm Black and I'm proud." In this case, race, as expressed through a specific cultural artifact, the music of James Brown, is used to justify an argument rooted in the political economy of class articulation in European society.

Using the "ghetto" or the "'hood" as the dominant metaphor, rap music has vividly presented this emphasis on the lower class. Whereas the earlier days of the genre were dominated by macho posturing, "dick" grabbing, and braggadocio, recently the thematic core of rap music has tended toward a narrative of life in the "'hood." With the advent of West Coast (primarily Los Angeles) rap, the life of a young African American male and his struggle to survive have become a recurrent theme, demonstrating firm entrenchment in the jungle-like setting known as the ghetto.[4] Rappers who resisted this emphasis were regarded as impostors of the tradition. Thus a concentration on class struggle has been central to defining the cutting edge of rap music during this phase.

The reliance on this now-clichéd narrative and the media's eager embrace of the ghetto lifestyle encouraged the eventual transformation of the "'hood" scenario from initially sublime to utterly ridiculous. Through an intense combination of media manipulation and artistic culpability, the issue of class struggle has been reduced to mere spectacle, as opposed to a sustained critical interrogation of domination and oppression. This genre of rap is becoming the modern-day equivalent of the 1970s "Blaxploitation" film, the earliest examples of which, works of African American grassroots financial struggle turned into valuable products of the culture, were duplicated, depoliticized, and ultimately rendered devoid of all cultural significance.

Rap represents the emotional range of urban, mostly male, existence. At the same time, the commodifying impulses of the music industry have opened a space for selling cultural products that in their very construction undermine the structure which distributes them. It is well known that rap's massive popular audience consists of dominant and marginal audiences. Nor is it a revelation that the capitalistic courting of this massive audience at some level solidifies the music's political message. However, there is a point at which radical political discourse meets the demands of the marketplace and the two merge. The space between the points where radical political discourse can critique dominant culture and dominant culture becomes financially viable through the selling of this contrary discourse is the only available space for a reasoned under-standing of contemporary political culture.

West's notion of a "politics of difference" sees the current cultural situation as indicative of an "inescapable double bind." This bind in-volves the reality of financial dependence that defines the structural dimension of rap music as a metaphorical "escape" from oppressive conditions, much like society's regard for African American professional athletes. The rapper, in this sense, is "simultaneously progressive and co-opted" (20).

Although a thin theoretical line separates radical political discourse in rap and the commodifying impulses of the dominant culture, our under-standing of popular culture requires that we critique both sides. Thus, the contemporary spectacle of the "ghetto" operates primarily to reinforce the dominant society's view of African American culture as a deprived wasteland. "Gangsta" rap offers original commentary on the horrific nu-ances of ghetto life. In many cases, what was once thought of as a radical critique of repressive state apparatuses, as in NWA's *Fuck tha Police*, has been transformed into a series of unapologetic narratives that celebrate violence, humiliate women, and indulge marijuana use to excess. Race and class struggle have become a series of rhetorical catch phrases and visual sign-posts absent of any political or social relevance. This overt rejection of poli-tics has now become a theme unto itself—one that is reflective of several larger issues.

Yet what many consider the redundant "nigga in the 'hood" scenario is actually much more complex. Instead of relying solely on this gangsta trend, a small core of rappers have continued to advance what was at one time thought of as a progressive political agenda which analyzes race, class, and in some cases gender through rigorous cultural critique. Foremost in this group of political rappers concerned with cultural politics are Public Enemy, Sister Souljah, KRS-One, and Arrested Devel-opment. A certain Afrocentric theme runs through each of the above, yet their individual positions cover a spectrum of topics related to living in late-twentieth-century American society. Nevertheless, none of these acts has had a record of any significance, financially or culturally, in quite some time.

As with the declining significance of Spike Lee as a political voice, though, and of the new Black aesthetic, these political rappers have not been able to link their progressive politics with the ever-changing demands of the music industry or the rap audience; thus their critiques have lately fallen on deaf ears, and their cultural significance has almost completely disappeared. Witness the breakup of the one-time leaders of this political trend, Public Enemy, in the summer of 1995. In contemporary culture it is not only important to bring the political noise, but one must remain significant from an audience perspective as well.

Progressive politics minus the ability to flow lyrically and pump out phat beats has no place in rap culture. This is not to diminish political rap, but to point out that we are analyzing music, as opposed to a rhetoric of pure politics. In addition, the definition of politics, or at least what is political, has changed as the various generational shifts and their class dispositions have occurred.

Arrested Development

The Atlanta-based rap group Arrested Development was the most interesting new act of 1992. The group's male and female members sing as well as rap, while their image is built around the wearing of dreadlocks and African-style clothing. This is in contrast to the image of both the "b-boy" of the East Coast and the West Coast gangsta. Arrested Development suggests a strong stylistic exception to conventions determined by the prevalence of the more popular East and West Coast images; they also can be easily linked with the politics of the new Black aesthetic.

Arrested Development shares its context with a segment of the contemporary African American collegiate audience who use African fashion and hairstyles to demonstrate their political connection to that continent. In this sense, fashion and style function as both icon and commodity. This emphasis on an Afrocentric style not only is a response to the monotonous fashions of other rappers, but also is a rejection of the conservative "preppie" image favored by a certain group of white collegiates, which took on added cultural currency during the Reagan/ Bush era. On the other hand, this emphasis on Afrocentricity in fashion becomes easily devalued as it is transformed into a mass commodity. This is the strong contention of Kobena Mercer, who suggests that hairstyles such as the afro and dreadlocks

> counter-politicized the signifier of ethnic devalorization, redefining blackness as a positive attribute, but on the other hand, perhaps not, because within a relatively short period both styles became rapidly depoliticized and, with varying degrees of resistance, both were incorporated into mainstream fashions in the dominant culture.
> (251)

This situation demonstrates, once again, the seemingly contradictory nature of political culture in the age of commodity fetishism. Signifiers of leftist political culture are easily corrupted as they are co-opted by the fashion industry of dominant society.

Musically, Arrested Development challenges the traditions of rap, the most visible difference being the use of singing in conjunction with the traditional rapping over beats (this singing style has since become quite popular). The group's songs address topics ranging from homelessness to the search for spirituality and African Americans' connection with Africa. Their popular appeal is demonstrated by their appearance as opening act on the 1992–93 En Vogue tour, the use of the song "Tennessee" as the theme for the short-lived NBC situation comedy *Here and Now*, their appearance as the only contemporary voice on the soundtrack for Lee's *Malcolm X* (1992), and their selection as both "Best New Artist" and "Best Rap Artist" at the 1993 Grammy Awards.

Arrested Development benefits from a series of other African American acts that have foregrounded a certain leftist bohemian political agenda. Arrested Development belongs to the musical tradition that includes the 1970s band Sly and the Family Stone—this group is sampled on "People Everyday"—the multicultural rhythm and blues group War, and most recently African American female folk singer Tracy Chapman. Yet, the combination of a derivative folk song content, politics associated with the peace movement, and rap is probably best exemplified by the rap organization Native Tongues, of which groups such as De La Soul and A Tribe Called Quest most easily demonstrate this pattern.[5]

A close analysis of Arrested Development's "People Everyday" song and video helps to reveal their political agenda. Using the sample from Sly Stone's track "Everyday People," Arrested Development argues for a kind of cultural innocence or purity. This notion of purity is exemplified through a juxtaposition of the harsh urban realities of the street prominent in contemporary rap and their embrace of the premodern "country" simplicity of a rural landscape. At one level the group attempts to be all-inclusive in its outlook, forwarding an Afrocentric version of political correctness that critiques race, class, and gender, as opposed to privileging the male-dominated discourse that rap has often been guilty of presenting. Yet in doing so the group offers a position that unintentionally erects a class hierarchy while simultaneously trying to destroy existing hierarchies.

The video's time frame spans one day, as marked by the rising of the sun at the beginning of the video and its setting at the conclusion. Thus we are alerted to the concern with time and the extent to which time and space function in defining African American politics. This concern with time is also evident in the title of the album, *3 Years, 5 Months, and 2 Days in the Life of Arrested Development.*

The video begins by calling on multiple aspects of the African oral tradition. Group member Headliner offers a verbal and visual address. After he announces who he is, we get an extreme close-up of his lips. In American society, lips have gone from a regressive stereotype that emphasized the excessive fullness of African American lips through numerous visual objects in American culture (Sambo pictures, lawn jockeys, etc.) to the current trend toward using this fullness as a visual demonstration of one's Africanness. White models and actresses appropriate these features through chemical or surgical treatment as a fashionable sign of what is considered beauty.[6] This modern-day example of exploitiveness is what bell hooks describes as "eating the other."

From this tight close-up, we move to a series of rapidly edited shots that alternate between Headliner's reggae-style call and visual images of the group's response. This visual dimension is edited to visually replicate the verbal call-and-response pattern that the group establishes. It also alternates between black and white and color images and privileges the oral as it motivates the visual direction of the iconography. Thus oral culture is used in conjunction with the character's motivation of visuals to create a stimulating African American music video.

Through another series of rapidly edited shots, we witness the group's reliance on a strongly rural agrarian aesthetic. Riding on the back of a pickup truck, the equally mixed group of male and female participants are shown in their loosely fitting cast-off–style African clothing, either with their hair in knotty dreadlocks or bald. This emphasis on the rural is supplemented by various shots of the wide-open landscape, dirt roads, wooden porches, and an idyllic series of visual icons that foreground the technologically untainted and morally empowered version of African American life that Arrested Development argues for throughout this album, and especially in the song "People Everyday."

As we witness little children running, playing, and riding their bicycles, and older people enjoying life in a variety of rural settings, we are also clued in to the political agenda that informs Arrested Development. The rejection of modernity that this visual setting evokes harks back to the "pre–New Negro" ideas of Booker T. Washington. These ideas embraced the virtues of southern pastoral living in opposition to the supposed utopic images of the industrialized North. Washington's argument suggested that the independence that was made possible through this rural lifestyle and economy was superior to the technologically mechanized economy that was taking hold in northern society. Washington's now-redundant phrase "Lay your buckets down where you are" clearly emphasizes his desire to see the South, in all its simplicity, as the preferred landscape of his contemporaries, and of future generations of African Americans as well.

The angst associated with the dilemma of migration as opposed to settling in the South has numerous other cultural manifestations, including blues singer Juke Boy Bonner's comically titled cut "I'm Going Back to the Country Where They Don't Burn the Buildings Down," soul singer Gladys Knight's hit "Midnight Train to Georgia," August Wilson's play *The Piano Lesson*, Julie Dash's film *Daughters of the Dust*, and Charles Burnett's *To Sleep with Anger*.

Arrested Development modernizes this argument in their first single, "Tennessee." In a video similar to "People Everyday," the group rhetorically engages in a quizzical and at times cynical exploration of African American existence in contemporary society. In a prayer-like address, they wonder aloud about their tenuous place in contemporary though problem-filled America: "Lord I've been really stressed / Down and out, losing ground / Although I am Black and proud / Problems got me pessimistic / Brothers and sisters keep messin' up / Why does it have to be so damn tough?"

The refrain of the song (and incidentally the portion used in the introduction to the short-lived sitcom *Here and Now*) suggests the possibility of freedom and understanding that lies ahead. Speech asks the Lord to "Take me to another place / Take me to another land / Make me forget all the hurt / Let me understand your plan." This spiritually informed intellectual journey, using "Tennessee" as the metaphor of freedom, is not unlike the musical excursions undertaken by John Coltrane during the latter part of his life and career. On the popular *A Love Supreme* and all of his later albums, Coltrane uses spirituality to express his intellectual and creative explorations.

In the same sense, Arrested Development sees "Tennessee" as a site of struggle that informs both past and present: "Walk the streets my forefathers walked / Climb the trees my forefathers hung from / Ask those trees for all their wisdom." According to Arrested Development, a return to these humble roots is necessary for an understanding of contemporary society and the place of the African American therein. This is evident in the lines "Now I see the importance of history / Why my people be in the mess that they be / Many journeys to freedom made in vain / By brothers on the corner playing ghetto games." At one level, Arrested Development offers a political impossibility. Their nostalgia for a romanticized version of early African American culture emphasizes the southern roots of existence, the absence of the modern, and a better quality of life. This seems not only simplistic but untenable considering the difficulties of this style of life within contemporary society. On another level, though, they are able to critique members of their own culture for assisting in the slow destruction of the culture.

Their intellectual posture foregrounds a globally leftist notion of Afrocentric discourse, and some would suggest that this takes rap music in a new direction. Arrested Development criticizes the way that contemporary society has destroyed positive aspects of a supposed earlier communal nature of African American culture, as well as exposed the self-inflicted problems associated with "brothers on the corner," a reference to the urge to romanticize urban Black male ghetto culture in other rap circles. A religiously self-critical orientation is strengthened by the presence of the group's spiritual advisor, Baba Oje, who allows for the emergence of an intellectually empowered voice that points to the future by invoking the past, as opposed to becoming ensconced in the trappings of the present.

Arrested Development's song and video for "People Everyday" extend the practice of self-critique within the African American community, in particular the function of women. The group advocates progressive gender politics, especially given the traditional male rap agenda. The female rappers/singers in the group have equal voice in defining its political project. This collaborative effort, like the critical academic endeavor undertaken by bell hooks and Cornel West in *Breaking Bread* (1991), demonstrates the possibilities of empowered political discourse that avoids the retreading of misogyny in favor of collective articulation.

During the extended call-and-response segment of "People Everyday," female rapper Aerle Taree responds to Speech's call. She often repeats the last part of his dialogue in order to strengthen her point. At the point where Speech refers to his passivity, "but I ain't Ice Cube," Aerle Taree asserts an unequivocal "Who?" This demonstrates the group members' dialectical self-consciousness regarding Ice Cube's political struggles as well as their reluctance to identify themselves with the militant posture of African American masculinity associated with Ice Cube. The female voice again becomes significant during the video's conclusion, when Montesho Eshe states the "moral" of the story. She summarizes the events and has the "last word," further exemplifying the group's progressive gender politics.

The focal point of "People Everyday" is the issue of gender. The members of Arrested Development, particularly Speech, are contrasted to what they define as a "group of brothers." Throughout the video we see black-and-white shots of African American males who personify media stereotypes of macho working-class behavior. We see this "group of brothers" holding forty-ounce bottles of malt liquor, grabbing their crotches, and laughing among themselves. When an African-attired Black woman approaches, they encircle her. After one of the men grabs her buttock, the others give him "dap" for displaying his masculinity.

The lyrics emphasize this obvious act of sexual harassment. "My day was going great and my soul was at ease / Until a group of brothers started buggin' out / Drinkin' the 40 oz. / Going the nigga route / Disrespecting my Black Queen / Holding their crotches and being obscene." Speech's reference to his "Black Queen" affirms the group's valorization of women.

This segment also demarcates the intellectual politics of Arrested Development from those of their lower-class counterparts, who display their masculine hostility toward African American women and other African Americans who do not fit into their lower-class stereotypes. This is evident in the proclamation that they came to "test speech cuz of my hairdo / And the loud bright colors that I wear, boo / I was a target cause I'm a fashion misfit / And the outfit that I'm wearing brothers dissin' it." Speech's African-themed appearance, and by extension his politics, are rejected by the "brothers" as unwelcome in their small ghettoized world. Much like the overpublicized Los Angeles gang culture of identification by "colors," the "brothers" in the video identify not only on the basis of race but on the basis of distinctive class stereotypes, the most prominent of which is clothing and appearance. Thus, like the gangbangers, the "brothers" are presented as destroying their own African American community through debauchery and violence.

This distinction between the politically correct behavior of Arrested Development and the "group of brothers" is based on the difference, according to Speech, between a "nigga" and an "African." In numerous media interviews, Speech defines a "nigga" as someone who realizes that he/she is oppressed and wallows in it; an "African" realizes his/her oppression and through knowledge attempts to overcome it. "Nigga" is often used by rappers who consider themselves products and practitioners of the ghetto life. The "hardest" and often the most confrontational rappers have defined themselves as "niggas" in opposition to the dominant society. For instance, NWA, having called their 1991 album *EFIL4SAGGIN* ("Niggas 4 Life" spelled backward), proclaim that "Real Niggas Don't Die"; Ice T boldly alerts his listeners that "I'm a nigga in America and I don't care what you are" and rejects "African American and Black" as inconsistent with his ghetto identity. Ice Cube has described himself as both "the nigga you love to hate" and "the wrong nigga to fuck wit." In each instance, "nigga" is politicized to indicate class as well as racial politics. This usage often involves a strong identification with the ghetto, but a regressive posture against women. "African" has recently been used to signify a spiritual connection with the continent and an Afrocentric political connection. Flavor Flav of Public Enemy has declared, "I don't wanna be called yo nigga" on the 1991 cut "Yo Nigga," which leads into Sister Souljah's assertion about "African people, too scared to call themselves African" on her 1992 cut "African Scaredy Cat in a One Exit Maze." Calling oneself African is supposed to demonstrate an advanced consciousness that eliminates any connection to America, and affirms one's links with an Afrocentric cultural, political, and spiritual base. Souljah suggests that those who reject this idea are "scared" to reject the ideological opposition that forces them to see America as home.

Arrested Development continually identify themselves as African in "People Everyday." Speech states, "I told the niggas please / Let us past friend / I said please cause I don't like killing Africans / But they wouldn't stop / & I ain't Ice Cube / Who? / But I had to take the brothers out for being rude!" Speech shows sympathy in his opposition to "niggas" by implying that they are ultimately "Africans." He also sees their masculine lower-class behavior as part of their definition as "niggas." Speech suggests that if they reject this class-based behavior, they can then be seen as "Africans." Yet in the end, they can aspire no higher than their lower-class status permits, as Speech declares, "That's the story yaw'll / Of a Black man / Acting like a nigga / And get stomped by an African!" This final statement emphasizes the contrast between "nigga" as defined by offensive behavior and African as defined by intellectual and political sophistication.

Much as in the confrontation scene in Lee's *School Daze* (1988) between the "fellas" and the men from the neighborhood at Kentucky Fried Chicken, Arrested Development enunciates class difference within the African American community, but they offer no critical analysis. Representations of class positions are reproduced through the reliance on this stereotyped behavior. Foregrounding this incident increases the possibility for it to replicate the dominant view of lower-class African American males as menacing.

Arrested Development brings an important intellectual and critical dimension to rap music and culture. It breaks away from the redundant "boy n the 'hood" scenario, which has become almost counterproductive through the media's overwhelming emphasis of it and the rap community's willingness to participate in such exploitation.

Arrested Development's female members are central to determining and articulating the group's political position. Their collaborative effort helps to provide an empowered position for female speakers without necessarily privileging the male voice. Unfortunately, in comparison to the rest of the rap community, the group's gender politics is uncommon.

Arrested Development's critical Afrocentricity involves an unconscious co-optation of regressive class politics. Through their sophisticated and at times self-righteous political position, they can critique modernity, capitalism, and gender. However, this position does not articulate an empowered position on class. Much like W. E. B. Du Bois's notion of the "talented tenth," Arrested Development attempts to close the societal gap on race, but widen it on class, and fails to engage in a political dialogue that could strengthen both areas. While Arrested Development does not blame the victim, they intensify class divisions with their intellectually elitist argument on the ghetto and African American male culture. While they claim to be concerned with "everyday people," it is obvious that they locate the "group of brothers" that they critique somewhere else. Yet as I asserted earlier, my interest in Arrested Development relates to how they open up the dialogue on politics and rap culture through the invocation of their gendered Afrocentric position. Thus multiple levels of political discourse can now be both demonstrated and juxtaposed within contemporary African American culture.

Arrested Development is clearly linked to a revisionist southern history, and they locate the problems of contemporary African American existence in the limits imposed by urbanization. This critical posture, in light of most other rap music, seems progressive and somewhat liberating. Yet when extrapolated to the larger themes just articulated, this position can be regarded as uncomplicated and ultimately mainstream. With conservative media manipulation of the popular term "political correctness" having all but cut this term off from its originally noble aspirations, Arrested Development can be easily viewed as aligned with this weakened position, as indicated by their public acceptability across race and gender lines. The group indicates in many ways the mainstreaming of Afrocentricity and the death of an earlier revolutionary agenda.

"But I Ain't Ice Cube!"

This limited political agenda, which is furthered by their inability to address the many class inequities in contemporary society, is best understood when comparing Arrested Development to their logical antithesis, Ice Cube, whose political agenda entails the iconic packaging of gangsta culture and the racialized urban American landscape—namely South Central L.A. In a sense, it is Ice Cube and what he represents that motivates much of Arrested Development's critical posture, as alluded to in the refrain "But I ain't Ice Cube" from "People Everyday." Ice Cube functions not only as an extension of the political argument in rap music, but also to expose the limitations of Arrested Development.

Ice Cube's strength lies in his ability to move easily between the general and the specific, simultaneously analyzing individual actions as well as societal oppression. Whereas Arrested Development can be seen in the same tradition as advocating an empowered version of religion, much like James Cone's idea of "Black Liberation Theology" or Albert Cleage's theory of the "Pan-African Orthodox," Ice Cube embraces the controversial tenets of Louis Farrakhan and the Nation of Islam. Unlike Arrested Development, who advocate a return to southern tradition as the solution to the problems of contemporary African American existence, Ice Cube's focus is the inner city in all its blighted glory.

Ice Cube's politics of location is clearly conversant with Burnett's *To Sleep with Anger.* Instead of focusing on the Deep South and the northward migration pattern of the early part of this century so often discussed in popular versions of African American history, Ice Cube, like Burnett, finds critical solace in a neglected segment of African American migration, the westward migration of southwestern (Arkansas, Louisiana, Texas) Blacks to Los Angeles primarily after World War II. Thus, Ice Cube's concerns with history are more contemporary, and in a sense better able to engage certain aspects of present-day culture. Whereas Arrested Development is interested in issues of modernity, Ice Cube is clearly associated with postmodernity.

This postmodern urban agenda is visually underscored through scenes in the "True to the Game" video of the burned-out remains of post-uprising Crenshaw Boulevard—a direct contrast to the rural landscapes that dominate Arrested Development's videos. Ice Cube sees African Americans' self-destruction and the propensity toward assimilating into mainstream society, thus losing one's identity, as the social hindrances to self-empowerment. Though these agenda items are not radically different from those advocated by Arrested Development, it is the urban setting, the embrace of the Nation of Islam, a postmodern criticism of societal institutions, and a rigorous critique of class politics that allow for a clear distinction between the two rap acts.

Ice Cube fuses these ideas into a coherent critical position on the album *Death Certificate,* which brings together the Nation of Islam's notion of race and a concern for the problems within African American society resulting from late commodity culture and the neoconservatism of the Reagan/Bush era. The album is equally divided between what Ice Cube describes as the "Death" and the "Life" sides. On the "Death" side, Ice Cube documents the violently destructive mentality of much of lower-class African American culture. Gangbanging, sexism, wanton violence, and other abusive behaviors are presented without the usual saccharine justification or uninformed rejection, but as harsh realities. This is what he wants to "kill." The "Life" side concerns revitalization and getting at the roots of these societal problems, dealing with them efficiently, and moving on to more concrete solutions.

The "Death" side begins with the funeral of another of Ice Cube's long line of "dead homiez." When Minister Khallid Muhammad of the Nation of Islam eulogizes the victim, he establishes the album's critical posture. Muhammad concludes by stating that the person being eulogized, who we know by this time is Ice Cube, was "the wrong nigga to fuck wit." It is at this point that Ice Cube begins his verbal assault on the racism, conformity, and overall lack of self-expression in contemporary society. Still seeing himself as the ultimate rebel who exists outside of both Black and white society, Ice Cube goes on a verbal rampage, attacking everything from contemporary African American popular music to police brutality. Much as in his opening declaration on *Amerikkka's Most Wanted*, "The Nigga You Love to Hate," Ice Cube revels in his utter disgust with American culture. African American complacency is as detrimental to progress as the most vile forms of white supremacy. Ice Cube's unrelenting attack on these cultural manifestations becomes the core of his identity: the angry Black man, the enraged lyricist.

At the conclusion of the "Death" side we are slowly transformed from sympathetic yet passive listeners into unconscious perpetrators of the very acts and attitudes that reinforce oppressive behavior. Once again, Ice Cube treats African Americans and the dominant society as equal culprits in the continual destruction of African American culture. Yet as the "Life" side begins with the cries of a newborn baby, we are given a glimpse of hope as to the future undoing of the shackles of oppression. Ice Cube implies through the metaphor of "life" that a strong critical, and at times self-critical, posture is necessary to fully understand the dynamics that restrict African American progress and ultimate empowerment in the larger society. The "Life" side proceeds with a critical analysis of sexual harassment, forced patriotism, assimilation, the self-destructive nature of gang violence, and the unwitting rejection of one's culture and soul for financial gain. The "Life" side takes Ice Cube's project to the next level, as he has successfully found a way to neither romanticize nor unequivocally reject the societal problems facing African Americans. Instead, he seems to have found a much-needed ground of critical scrutiny with useful extrapolation for the future. As underscored below by Khallid Muhammad's sermon, the implications of "life" for future directions become the source of potential empowerment.

> No longer dead, deaf, dumb, and blind
> Out of our mind
> Brainwashed with the white man's mind
> No more homicide!
> No more fratricide, genocide, or suicide!
> Look the goddamn white man in his cold blue eyes
> Devil don't even try
> We like Bebe's kids
> We don't die
> We multiply
> You've heard the death side
> So open your black eyes to the resurrection, rebirth, and rise.

In Ice Cube's use of Muhammad's oratorical qualities, Nation of Islam icons ("blue-eyed devil") are fused with icons of the gang subculture ("we don't die, we multiply") and popular African American media culture (Robin Harris's "Bebe's kids") to create an empowered rhetorical articulation that points toward the possibility of a future free of these restraints. Muhammad also relies on a liberatory notion of freedom as expressed through popular religious icons (resurrection, rebirth, and rise), giving new meaning to the at times constraining position that organized religion has always occupied for African Americans. Thus, the "Life" side places contemporary African American culture under a critical microscope, while refusing to relinquish the nature of dominant culture as it separates and ultimately destroys the fabric of African American society.

Central to Ice Cube's political agenda is a critique of the nihilism that exists throughout lower-class African American society. In conjunction with Cornel West's argument in *Race Matters*, where this nihilism is seen in the form of "psychological depression, personal worthlessness, and social despair" (13), Ice Cube, in the provocative tune, "Us," vividly extents this argument by discussing the contradictory nature of African

American culture as it often assumes a posture of victimized helplessness. "Sometimes I believe the hype, man / We mess it up ourselves and blame the white man."

In a society where conservative political criticism of African Americans is abundant and encourages a defensive posture that romanticizes societal problems, Ice Cube has rejected the idea of the "airing of one's dirty laundry in public"—or to use the more succinctly Black phrase, "putting one's business in the street"—in favor of exposing the problems of the community for public debate. This rejection of victimization for an empowered critical agenda goes against the grain of African American public etiquette. But unlike conservative African American critics such as Clarence Thomas, Stanley Crouch, and Shelby Steele, Ice Cube takes a position that cannot be easily co-opted. He uses this self-critical posture as an instance of cultural empowerment. His analysis of race and emphasis on class opens up the dialogue on the problems of contemporary culture, as opposed to closing off this debate through a needed, but often uninformed, cultural deconstruction.

This self-critical duality is exemplified through Ice Cube's commentary on drugs and the subculture within which drugs circulate.

> And all y'all dope dealers
> You as bad as the police
> Cause you kill us
> You got rich when you started slingin' dope
> But you ain't built us a supermarket
> So we can spend our money with the blacks
> Too busy buying gold and Cadillacs.

The nightly news is full of stories about the entrenchment of drugs in the African American community and the ghettoized culture that breeds this behavior. Conservatives argue that local dealers should be treated as felons and be given the death penalty. It is no surprise that many African Americans who live in the midst of what amounts to an open-air drug market corroborate elements of this conservative argument out of sheer necessity, as their lives are in constant danger.

On the other hand, in the gangsta rap community from which Ice Cube emerged, many glamorize the lifestyle and economic independence of the drug dealer. Rapper Scarface has even rejected the usual female sexual subservience by stating, "Fuck the bitches / I want money and the power" to demonstrate his complicity with the excesses of late commodity capitalism within the drug culture.

Ice Cube is careful not to fall into either ideological trap as he turns his critique of the drug culture into a positive vision for the community. The drug dealer's embrace of the fetishized commodity—gold and Cadillacs—is seen as hindering an economically informed Black nationalism that allows African Americans to spend their capital within their own self-sufficient communities. Drug dealing is not condemned in terms of "family values" but, as in the case of Gordon Parks Jr.'s *Superfly* (1972), is seen as an imposed necessity that can potentially be turned into an economic means of cultural empowerment.

Ice Cube goes on in "Us" to enunciate the contradictory nature of much within the African American community:

> Us gonna always sing the blues
> Cause all we care about is hair styles and tennis shoes
> If you mess with mine
> I ain't frontin'
> Cause I'll beat you down like it ain't nothin'
> Just like a beast
> But I'm the first nigga to holler out, peace
> I beat my wife and children to a pulp
> When I get drunk and smoke dope
> Got a bad heart condition
> Still eat hog mauls and chitlins
> Bet my money on the dice or the horses
> Jobless
> So I'm a hoe for the armed forces
> Go to church but they tease us
> With a picture of a blue-eyed Jesus
> Used to call me Negro
> After all this time I'm still bustin' up the chiferow.

His claim that African Americans engage with oppressive economic and cultural forces by an overemphasis on style and commodity culture reflects how corporations target African Americans as the prime market for their products. The Nike/Michael Jordan advertisements are probably the most popular, with the Gatorade slogan "I want to be like Mike" furthering the link between stylish commodity and African American culture. With other shoe companies having entered the fray, ads for athletic shoes are located in an urban environment dominated by African Americans. The proliferation of such products in music videos makes increasingly apparent how mediated slices of African American life have become oversaturated with stylish commodities.

Ice Cube argues that the suturing effects of commodity culture cause those who are oppressed to lose sight of their oppression as a result of this willing yet uncritical relationship with the dominant society. The "singing of the blues" is a direct result of this uneasy identity with popular elements of the dominant culture. African American identity is depoliticized as possessing commodities becomes superior to knowing the political dynamics that fuel consumption.

Witness the recent fashion for the letter *X* on baseball caps and clothing. Originally created as an endorsement for Spike Lee's film about Malcolm X, the letter has become a vulgar postmodern reification of what Jean Baudrillard described as simulation, where signs are detached from all referents and exist simply as signs. A knowledge of Malcolm X, his life, and his philosophies is no longer required. The *X* stands for all of the above and simultaneously allows those wearing it to demonstrate their cultural hipness and their stylish political agenda. Ultimately, the *X* loses all association with Malcolm and simply becomes the sign of popular commodity culture. Regardless of a wearer's politics, it becomes the moment's most fashionable statement.

In addition to pointing out the many contradictions of African American life, Ice Cube offers several examples of gaps in relation to the dominant society. His political agenda stresses public self-criticism to force African Americans to deal with internal problems and not use racism as an answer to all questions of oppression. While he acknowledges that racism exists and should not be ignored, he suggests that it often is exacerbated through an uncritical relationship with commodity culture and other self-destructive activities. Ice Cube moves between conservative and liberal positions in making this assertion. The fact that an African American popular figure, albeit a self-proclaimed nationalist, has taken this stance through a strong cultural product opens up a dialogue that allows for solutions to the difficulties imposed by late white supremacist capitalist culture.

Ice Cube also sees another problem facing African American empowerment: attempts to assimilate into mainstream society, especially when it involves compromising one's cultural identity. In a sophisticated class critique, assimilation into middle-class existence is portrayed as consistent with oppression. This argument is clearly articulated through the song and video "True to the Game."

The most informative of Ice Cube's arguments about compromising one's identity appears in the metaphor of musical assimilation—the tendency of many rappers to reject the genre's hard political edge for success in mainstream culture. In Ice Cube's video we see a rapper dressed in what is coded as hard-core clothing—a skullcap, sweatshirt, and work khakis—slowly dissolve into an entertainer attired in red sequins who smiles repeatedly and performs elaborate dance moves. While the immediate reference is pop star Hammer—who in his recent comeback has contradicted his earlier self by embracing gangsta culture—the video implicates all who use the ghettoized trappings of hardcore rap to facilitate their transition into the more lucrative musical mainstream.

The transition from hard-core rapper to pop star is at the expense of one's cultural and class identity. The rapper attempts to change his style for the sake of mainstream culture, only to be exploited and ultimately rejected.

> On MTV
> But they don't care
> They'll have a new nigga next year
> Out in the cold
> No more white fans and no more soul
> And you might have a heart attack
> When you find out black folks don't want you back
> And you know what's worst?
> You was just like the nigga in the first verse
> Stop sellin' out your race
> And wipe that stupid ass smile off your face
> Niggas always gotta show they teeth
> Now I'm gonna be brief
> Be true to the game.

While Black Entertainment Television (BET) and the Miami-based video jukebox THE BOX have long featured African American music videos, receiving play on cable network MTV is now seen as the ultimate mark of crossover success. Ironically, it was only recently, after much initial reservation, that MTV began playing African American music on a regular basis. Though programs such as Yo MTV Raps and MTV Jams are popular, it is the cable station's association with rock and roll and heavy metal that has made it a symbol of mainstream white culture in the music industry.

Ice Cube's assertion that "they don't care" directly comments on the long-standing exploitive nature of the music industry, as recently exemplified by MTV, and how it has historically used African American culture as trendy and disposable material: "they'll have a new nigga next year." Ice Cube also suggested that once the assimilative rapper, characterized by an excessive smile, has been rejected by mainstream culture, the African American cultural community will have no further need for him. In this sense these rappers, and by extension the desire to assimilate in any form, function as complicit in their own oppression.

Ice Cube has demonstrated through both "Us" and "True to the Game" an empowered class critique of nihilistic individuals as well as societal institutions. This critique is furthered by his continual use of Nation of Islam ideology. Historically the Nation of Islam has been a solid avenue of empowerment for individuals who exist outside mainstream society, in African American society as well as in society as a whole. Their focus on convicts, ex-convicts, and reformed drug abusers, especially African American males, is without equal. Nation of Islam patriarch Elijah Muhammed clearly foregrounds this in the title of his popular book, *Message to the Black Man.* It is no coincidence that Ice Cube's manipulation of this ideology, with the trappings of L.A. gang culture, can forward an empowered critique of those things which entrap the lower-class Black male. The gaps in Arrested Development's elitist critical agenda are here fully exposed.

Yet the limitations to Ice Cube's project lie in the same arena as does his strength. Though the Nation of Islam can critique bourgeois Black society, it cannot empower those who exist outside of the underclass that it so effectively targets. The xenophobic anti-intellectualism and the passive approach to critically engaging mainstream society while existing in it are the point at which this form of critique loses its usefulness. These are the limitations that forced Malcolm X, a true intellectual, to leave the Nation of Islam in search of wisdom elsewhere. And while Ice Cube's clever fusion of Nation of Islam ideology with gangsta iconography is an important form of class critique, it cannot take the questions of race and class to the next level of understanding.

The strength of the Nation of Islam has always been its ability to erect a solid image of defiance. While this is a useful tool in a people's rise to consciousness, defiance should not be the embodiment of all political understanding. If in contemporary society an embrace of the Nation of Islam, which has always been misunderstood as an empowered expression of Black nationalism, is the extent of our historical knowledge, then we are truly at an intellectual impasse. Ice Cube's, and the Nation's, refusal to properly engage a gender critique notwithstanding, it is the limitation of their class critique that ultimately leaves much to be desired.

Much of the political dimension that for a brief period defined rap music, and by extension African American popular culture, has been effectively killed off. Discussions of the resurgence of Black nationalism or attempts to define the elusive term "Afrocentricity" have subsided; in their place we began to hear discussions about the rights to linguistic property: "niggas," "bitches," "hoes," etc. We also began to hear denouncements of the hyperviolent atmosphere surrounding gangsta culture, which eventually led to congressional hearings on the impact that this nihilism is having at a societal level.

The fact that these issues would move outside the rap world into the United States Congress attests to the magnitude of this culture in the larger society. Yet it also wrongly reasserts the "moral imperative" of African American criticism, which has often been the rallying cry for a problematic censorship under the guise of "what's good for our children," as in the critical rejection of a film such as Melvin Van Peebles's *Sweetsweetback's Badass Song* (1971) on these grounds. While these moralistic cries shed no light on the real issues that underlie a systematic suturing of self-hatred with which African Americans have been forced to identify, rap music, in this sense of a new cultural politics, has been a vehicle for the expression of multiple voices—such as Arrested Development and Ice Cube—that have always had difficulty being heard. The real question becomes, When will there be a sustained movement that examines this historical self-hatred, while linking both politics and culture in a way that truly empowers all who subscribe to a liberated notion of existence in an otherwise oppressive society? These concerns clearly prompt Ice Cube's self-critical imperative to "check yo self, before you wreck yo self."

A Small Introduction to the "G" Funk Era: Gangsta Rap and Black Masculinity in Contemporary Los Angeles

THREE

> Damn, I'm such a "G," it's pathetic.
>
> —Ice Cube, "Down for Whatever"

In a relatively short period of time, American popular culture has witnessed a radical shift away from Bill Cosby's prominent image of Black masculinity, which seemed to define the 1980s. In less than ten years, the most visible representation of African American maleness, which was previously defined by wealth, status, and what many would call an overall "positive" image, has been transformed into an oppositional image, which exists in poverty, remains marginal, and is characterized by what many have called "the scum of the earth" in a colloquial sense, but which fits more closely with the idea of "the truly disadvantaged." I am specifically referring to the image of the gangsta and his embodiment in the cultural medium of gangsta rap.

The focus of this chapter is the cultural context that defines gangsta rap, with specific attention to the issues of historical significance, the furthering of the oral tradition, the cultural currency of Blackness, the primacy of visual imagery, a mediated aesthetic known as the hyperreal, and how these issues come together around the larger dilemma of Black masculinity and its relationship to modern-day Los Angeles.[1] Included in this discussion will be attempts to address the differences between African American folk culture and popular culture; the resistant anti-authoritarianism of gangsta rap, which has involved even the FBI; and the declining significance of overtly political discourse in rap in the era of gangsta rap.

"L.A. proved too much for the man," Gladys Knight sang some time ago, and though she was talking about a fictional character who had tired of the urban sprawl of Los Angeles and longed for the peace of a mythic Georgia, her words fit quite well with the contemporary phenomenon of gangsta rap. Los Angeles informs a great deal of Black popular culture—be it the Hughes brothers' use of the Watts riots to begin *Menace II Society* or Dr. Dre's use of various voices from the civil unrest of 1992 on the track "The Day the Niggaz Took Over"—necessitating an analysis of this city and its influence on the cultural artifacts that emerge from it.

Gangsta Rap: From the Marginal to the Popular

> Here's a little somethin' 'bout a nigga like me
> Never shoulda been let out the penitentiary
> Ice Cube
> And I'd like to say
> That I'm a crazy motherfucker from around the way
> Since I was a youth
> I smoke weed out
> Now I'm the kinda nigga that you read about
> Taking a life or two
> That's what the hell I do
> You don't like how I'm living
> Well, fuck you!
> This is a gang
> and I'm in it
> and I'm gonna fuck you up in a minute . . .
> Cause I'm the kinda nigga that's built to last
> Fuck wit me
> I'll put my foot in your ass.
>
> —NWA, "Gangsta, Gangsta"

These explicit declamatory lines demonstrate the dominant thematic sentiment of defiant lower-class Black ultramasculinity that permeates the genre of "gangsta" rap. The album *Straight outta Compton* (1988), from which the Niggaz Wit Attitude (NWA—a group consisting of Ice Cube, Easy E, Dr. Dre, MC Ren, and DJ Yella)—track is taken, marked the public inauguration of material that would come to extend beyond traditional musical or generic conventions.

The initial underground popularity of this music, set in place by NWA, would come to situate an entire cultural movement. Even at this early stage, the Federal Bureau of Investigation targeted NWA and their song "Fuck tha Police," from this same album, as subversive and threatening. This gesture furthered the masculine mystique and allure of gangsta rap in a genre that relies on embellishing the menacing quality so often associated with the urban lumpenproletariat. What better way to demonstrate one's position as a true "menace to society" than by having one's lyrics cited as threatening by the highest echelon of government law enforcement?

In the parlance of the street, men are praised, with phallic connotations, for their ability to be "hard"; this is a modern-day variation on what used to be referred to as "cool." In order to be hard, one must maintain a state of detached defiance, regardless of the situation. By clearly enunciating societal defiance, the lyrics to "Gangsta, Gangsta" reference a direct trajectory from the earliest days of African American folklore as expressed through oral culture. There has always been a proverbial "bad nigga" who, in serving notice of his presence, was feared by all around him—white people as well as people in his own community. Whether characterized by the images of Jack Johnson, Bigger Thomas, or the legendary Dolemite, it is apparent that rap music, especially gangsta rap, has successfully drawn on this tradition and rearticulated it for a contemporary audience.[2]

Following in the tradition of the "bad nigga," we can see how the FBI's misguided gesture in the case of NWA inadvertently helped sustain the defiant posture of masculine aggression that would constitute much of the thematic foundation from which gangsta rap would evolve.

> Creep with me
> As I crawl through the hood
> Maniac, lunatic
> Call me Snoop Eastwood
> Kickin' dust as I bust
> Police
> and

> You never hear me talkin' bout peace . . . Yeah
> and you don't stop
> Cause it's 1–8–7 on an undercover cop.
>
> —Dr. Dre and Snoop Doggy Dogg, "Deep Cover"

This quotation, taken from the soundtrack of Bill Duke's *Deep Cover* (1992), links gangsta rap with the medium of cinema. Black music has always informed cinematic representations of African American culture, and at this historical juncture gangsta culture began moving from a position not unlike folk culture to a more public place in American popular culture. This lyric also shows how gangsta rap culture is influenced by Hollywood images of excess, and in turn Hollywood is able to appropriate and merchandise the visual imagery conveyed through gangsta rap.

Integral to this transition from folk culture to popular culture and the importance therein of the visual have been Dr. Dre and his partner in crime, Snoop Doggy Dogg. They have been the primary catalysts in mainstreaming gangsta culture into contemporary society. Dr. Dre, who had an album that spent close to a year (from late 1992 until the fall of 1993) in the top five and went multi-platinum in terms of sales, and who had three videos in regular rotation on MTV, represents a radical departure from the days, some two to three years earlier, when Ice Cube's first solo effort, *Amerikkka's Most Wanted* (1990), with no radio or video airplay, went gold in five days.

While Ice Cube's unparalleled success, relative to the dictates of contemporary marketing strategies in the music business, suggests an almost utopic underground circuit of African American listenership, Dr. Dre's and subsequently Snoop's popularity in mainstream society represents the growth of gangsta culture into a pop cultural force with few competitors. It also demonstrates how Blackness, especially in the form of hardened Black masculinity, has become a significant commodity in contemporary popular culture.

In the past, this popularity would have been a sure sign of accommodation, as the music would have to be compromised in some major way in order to be made mainstream. Gangsta rap has come to prominence because of its unwillingness to do so. The music and culture industries have found ways to sell this extreme nonconformity, while many rappers have successfully packaged their mediated rage for a mass audience. Audience members of all races use the music as a form of resistance or rebellion, with the truly disadvantaged Black male serving as the supreme representative of adolescent angst, minority disenfranchisement, and an overall sense of cynicism about American society. Thus gangsta rap provides a vehicle for cathartic expression well beyond an exclusively Black space.

On the heels of the subversive mystique generated by the FBI inquisition, Dr. Dre would go on to demonstrate not only that this masculine defiance could threaten virtually every aspect of society but, more important, that it could cross over to the mass audience. Hardened images of defiant masculinity have always had a strong appeal in American culture—e.g., John Wayne, Edward G. Robinson—but this sort of imagery is seldom associated with Black males.

While Black males have always epitomized masculine subversiveness in regard to the larger society, rarely does this ethos, which emanates from a specifically lower-class Black male perspective, result in commercial success without thematic compromises being made along the way. As a matter of fact, it is the extreme nature of the performance that substantiates the value of this cultural form for the rappers and their audience. However, this unadulterated Black cultural product is often sold to people whose racial and social circumstances are the complete opposite of those producing it. This situation allows the most marginal representatives of African American folk culture to achieve financial success, albeit primarily for the white-owned music companies. The financial profit also allows for the continued dissemination of a truly disadvantaged perspective via the mainstream media.

> I had no idea of peace and tranquillity. From my earliest recollections there has been struggle, strife, and the ubiquity of violence. . . . I've always felt like a temporary guest everywhere I've been, all of my life, and, truly, I've never been comfortable. Motion has been my closest companion, from room to room, house to house, street to street, neighborhood to neighborhood, school to school, jail to jail, cell to cell—from one man-made hell to another. So I didn't care one way or another about living or dying—and I cared less than that about killing someone.
>
> —Monster Kody, Eight Trey Gangsta Crips, Monster (1993)

This statement by former gang member Monster Kody of the notorious Eight Trey Gangsta Crips of South Central Los Angeles clearly blurs the line between fact and fiction. What Ice Cube, Dr. Dre, and Snoop have fictionalized through their highly stylized narratives of gang culture, Monster has rendered in autobiography, thus linking these contemporary concerns to the historical by using a form that embodies such relevant tradition for the overall understanding of African American culture.

The 1993 publication of Monster's memoirs, *Monster: The Autobiography of an L.A. Gang Member*, represented the solidification of the gangsta genre as a cultural movement in contemporary American society. This movement had now evolved from regional association, through the heights of media-generated popularity, to an assumed cultural sophistication which could be conferred only by the substantiation of this lifestyle in literary form. The gangsta genre had now moved into a multi-mediated arena that defied charges of trendiness or simple exploitation. The movement had effectively become an integral part of both African American culture and American popular culture.

Monster details the nuances of gang life in South Central Los Angeles from the mid-1970s to the present. The impending publication of the text was the subject of both an extended *Esquire* and a *Los Angeles Times Magazine* feature in the spring of 1993, some three months prior to the release of the hardback edition. In the introduction to the *L.A. Times* piece, Michelle Wallace asks, "How did an Eight-Trey Gangster Crip named Monster go from hoodlum to literary hot property?" The answer entails a quest toward understanding the culture industry's embrace of gangsta iconography and society's fascination with this most recent version of gangsters in American society. The publication of Monster's memoirs demonstrated that this area of culture, in addition to its public popularity, should be regarded as an important commentary on the state of contemporary urban postindustrial existence for lower-class African American males. The literary reification of gangsta culture through Monster Kody's autobiography forced us once again to take "seriously" those voices which operate on the margins of society.

Monster's statement captures the point at which the image of the gangsta had evolved into a "cultural movement" which would include music, film, video, and, most important, literature as a legitimating strategy consistent with societal notions of artistic and political credibility. Consistent with the notion of a cultural movement are the repeated concerns that define my interest in gangsta rap culture: the issue of Black masculinity, in terms of both race and class, the dissemination of oral culture, and the importance of understanding Blackness as a commodity.

These conditions are taken to another level where the dictates of corporate entertainment culture serve as a backdrop for the massive dissemination of these images via mainstream channels of distribution. Many would suggest that mainstream society has once again exploited Black culture for its own purposes, in this case using the image of the gangsta to stereotype Black males as pathologically aggressive while laughing all the way to the bank. Yet this sentiment fails to incorporate the changes that have occurred surrounding the cultural production of

"Blackness" in the post–civil rights era, especially as they relate to the truly disadvantaged position.

Cash Rules Everything around Me

Sittin' in my living room
Calm and collected
Feelin' that gotta-get-mine perspective.

—Dr. Dre, "The Day the Niggaz Took Over"

Contemporary society has allowed the limited participation of African Americans in mainstream culture so long as it remains profitable to certain corporate interests. On the other hand, many African American performers and producers openly embrace this most recent form of "exploitation" so long as it provides them with the material possessions that make them more comfortable in an otherwise uncomfortably racist world.

Gangsta rap, with its themes of excess, takes the notion of "gettin' paid" or "gettin' mine" to its most extreme form. Dr. Dre provides an interesting example of this mentality in "The Day the Niggaz Took Over." In a previous generation, the tune's title would have been a declaration of nationalistic intent; here, "taking over" has to do with acquiring material possessions by any means necessary. Dre begins the tune by re-creating the atmosphere of the L.A. riots of April 1992 through the angry voices of those who were on the streets during this event—after which he declares his own disposition regarding the true politics of the riot, "Sittin' in my living room / Calm and collected / Feeling that gotta-get-mine perspective." Thus the riots are defined here not as a political reaction to the verdicts in the Rodney King case but as an opportunity to obtain material possessions through looting. This is furthered by Snoop's rhetorical refrain, "How many niggaz are ready to loot?"

Cornel West argues that much of the decline in the Black community can be attributed to "fortuitous and fleeting moments preoccupied with getting over—with acquiring pleasure, property, and power by any means necessary" (Race Matters, 5). He defines the contemporary cultural climate as "a market culture dominated by gangster mentalities and self-destructive wantonness," which pervades all of Black society, but "its impact on the disadvantaged is devastating, resulting in the violence of everyday life." Clearly the politics of gangsterism has come to replace the strong nationalist sentiment that would have defined previous political endeavors. According to West, this gangsta ethos functions as "the lived experience of coping with a life of horrifying meaninglessness, hopelessness, and lovelessness. The frightening result is a numbing detachment from others and a self-destructive disposition toward the world" (14).

This nihilistic sentiment is echoed by Snoop in the opening to Dr. Dre's *The Chronic* when he declares that gangsta culture is represented by "niggas wit big dicks, AK's, and 187 skills." Excess and oppressed Black masculinity are expressed symbolically through an exaggerated phallus, high-powered weaponry, and the ability to kill at will, which do much more than simply fulfill the societal stereotype of the threatening Black male. Instead, it can be argued that they deny the white supremacist denigration embodied in the stereotype and reverse the impact so as to become a purveyor of Black rage.

Yet, as the underside of this perversity continually leads to the obvious marginalization of Black women, it also has some connection to the continued extermination of lower-class Black males. We have seen the death of politics and the emergence of nihilism as the ruling order of the day. It is this sentiment that defines much of gangsta rap, certainly as it has entered mainstream culture. While this is the most obvious shortcoming of the genre itself, we cannot ignore the extent to which excess informs gangsta rap and culture, both thematically and in terms of an overall image. Acknowledging these societal tragedies is important, but there are concerns that constitute much of the public dialogue about race, class, and masculinity. A shift in focus to the thematic of excess, relative to the accumulation of capital and commodity and on the personal level, can contribute to an interesting discussion of the cultural elements of this situation.

On one hand, the excessive embrace of capital, sexism, and violence and a generally nihilistic mentality can be seen as the strident pathology of gangsta culture. Yet a critical distance is needed that moves away from traditional analysis. It is important to focus on how these issues reverberate within postmodern American culture, specific to the African American experience. These social issues cannot be ignored, yet the focal point becomes representation, especially as it is configured in a visual sense, and how the question of excess or spectacle redefines our understanding of these issues in contemporary society.

While I am careful not to minimize the impact of racism or to fall into the posture of "blaming the victim," I am suggesting that we shift our attention to the issue of racial representation in a postmodern society and how it affects the articulation of Blackness in popular culture. I am advocating a move away from the moralistic dimensions of African American cultural criticism, and toward an emphasis on capital, commodity, and how personal responsibility plays into the overall understanding of gangsta culture.

The Visual, with Los Angeles as Metaphor

The representation of gangsta culture is now prevalent throughout America, a far cry from the days when the music was heard only being played at local swap meets and being sold from the trunks of cars, when it was present only in the various "'hoods" of South Central Los Angeles, Watts, Compton, Long Beach, and Inglewood. DJ Quik's 1992 single "Just Lyke Compton" is a comical reflection on the impact of gangsta rap on various sectors of American society that would usually be considered immune to influences deriving from the regional confines of South Central L.A.

Quik describes the responses of several cities (Oakland, St. Louis, San Antonio, and Denver) to the spectacle of mediated gangsta culture. He details his encounters with several imitation gangstas in the course of his concert tour who had adopted the media-generated imagery of the culture without the history or personal experience that marks one as a participant in it. "I don't think they know / They too crazy for they own good / They need to stop watching that *Colors* and *Boyz n the Hood* / Too busy claimin' 60's / Tryin' to be raw / And never even seen the Shaw." Here he suggests that the impact of gangsta culture, most effectively demonstrated through references to popular films, has misled those who use this imagery as a model for ultramasculinity, making associations with gang-specific areas of Los Angeles (Rolling 60s/Crenshaw) that they have never inhabited. It is as if the media presentation of these areas is a substitute for the actual experience of having been there.

In other words, Compton, a convenient metaphor for the entirety of gangsta culture, came to affect large sectors of society though very few knew the specific circumstances that had created the aura around this area in the first place. As supported by NWA's evolutionary *Straight outta Compton*, Quik asks rhetorically, "How could a bunch of niggaz in a town like this have such a big influence on niggaz so far away?" The perpetrators, having blurred the line between the mediated life of a surreal Compton and their own real lives, have fallen under the suturing effects of mainstream representation. Real lives have been lost as a result of the violent associations with the image of "Compton," which in actuality is quite a small part of the vast landscape of Los Angeles.

By calling attention to the media spectacle surrounding the metaphoric image of Compton, Quik is arguing for authenticity, and a historically specific, geographically based understanding of gangsta culture, while critiquing the massive dissemination of this imagery without the requisite knowledge base. Yet as time would pass, mainstream media representation would make Quik's concerns about as comical as the recurrent themes in his song.

Gangsta, or "G," culture is the context within which "gangsta" rap flourished and is very specific to the late 1980s and early 1990s. The cultural movement is also geographically specific to the West Coast, especially Los Angeles. We have witnessed a proliferation of what I call the "articulation of Black Los Angeles," as the musings of gangsta culture fit neatly into a developing pattern that also includes the films of Charles Burnett, the gritty revisitation of the hard-boiled, noir literary genre from a Black perspective specific to writer Walter Mosley, and critical reflections on being Black in Los Angeles by Lynell George in *No Crystal Stair.*

This movement surrounding gangsta culture takes its representational cues from 1970s African American cultural production, thematically referencing the complex and contradictory nature of urban, lower-class Black male existence in a racist and nihilistic society. This culture is composed of fictional as well as real-life occurrences, mediated as well as nonmediated events. It is both real and imaginary, often at the same time. This culture involves the media of music, television, film, video, literature, and the lives of everyday people. It is, in a word, postmodern: a series of events that could have happened when they did specific only to the societal currents that define our existence.

Ain't no Future in Yo Frontin':
The Issue of Cultural Authenticity

Another side of the argument exposed through the lyrics of DJ Quik supports the idea that the visual has become prevalent as a way of understanding the reproduction of African American culture. In a February 3, 1994, *Wall Street Journal* front-page story entitled "How a Nice Girl Evolved into Boss, the Gangster Rapper," reporter Brett Pulley contrasts the real-life background of Lichelle Laws with her gangsta rap image known as Boss. He details her Catholic education along with her study of ballet, modern dance, and the piano, all signs of a middle-class upbringing—and a stark contrast to her new persona as Boss, one of the first and most successful female gangsta rappers in a genre not only dominated by men, but with a misogynist undercurrent. Pulley sees the two sides of life as being incompatible; one cannot simultaneously be a middle-class female and a gangsta.

What Pulley fails to understand, though, in line with our general infatuation with visual spectacle, is that image, whether real or fictional, is the defining characteristic of contemporary society, especially in gangsta culture. In a sense, the image of Boss the rapper, a hardened violent female on a murderous warpath, obliterates the real-life circumstances that may have defined her existence previously. It is not as though Boss conceals this luxurious past, as we hear her mother's voice lamenting the loss of her "little girl" from the answering machine on the opening track of her debut album, *Born Gangstaz.*

Boss's new image reflects a sort of conversion experience in which her middle-class upbringing is rejected for the more visually alluring experiences she describes, such as sleeping on park benches, slinging dope, and hanging out with gangbangers in the process of trying to get a record deal. Through these personal narratives, Boss is arguing for her place in a ghettoized world we have come to regard as "real."

This placement defines the necessary qualifications for participation in a genre where poverty and violence go hand in hand. Here the challenge toward authenticity and spectacle coalesce. This celebrated transition from middle-class princess to lower-class female gangsta is best expressed through a line from her first single, "Deeper," in which she details her journey "tryin' to get to Watts, but I'm stuck in Baldwin Hills." Watts, the ghetto enclave that formerly defined a large segment of lower-class Black Los Angeles existence, and which has recently become populated by as many equally distressed Latinos, is seen as preferable to the bourgeois trappings of Baldwin Hills, the area often described as the "Black Beverly Hills." Boss's reversal of desired class affiliation is a further endorsement of the importance of image in understanding the contemporary phenomenon of gangsta culture in a visually literate postmodern landscape. The image of the gangsta has taken the place of the "real"-life circumstances of Boss's middle-class childhood.

Gangsta Rap and the Hyperreal

This fascination with the image has become one of the thematic hallmarks of this genre. Much as with Jean Baudrillard's description of the hyperreal, a situation where the "contradiction between the real and the imaginary is effaced" (142), we can see in gangsta rap the continued blurring of the line between fiction and nonfiction. The alleged criminal activities of rappers Dr. Dre, Tupac Shakur, and Snoop

Doggy Dogg have received a great deal of media attention. At one time Dr. Dre had five different court dates pending on as many different charges, all having to do with some violent behavior, including his attack on female rap talk show host Dee Barnes. Tupac Shakur was also convicted of a number of crimes during his storied life. He was shot several times on his way to a recording studio in 1994 but survived. He died in September 1996, however, as the result of another shooting, this time following a Mike Tyson fight in Las Vegas.

Most notable, though, is the acquittal on murder charges of Snoop, who, like Tupac, represents a musical genre that often celebrates a gun culture gone crazy. Snoop's track "Murder Was the Case" sounds almost like an account of his real-life exploits. His performance of this tune on the 1994 MTV video awards concluded with a bold declaration of "I'm innocent, I'm innocent," bringing even more confusion about whether he was referring to the song itself or his own murder case, the fiction of the song or the reality of his life.

What is important here for the sake of analysis, in addition to the actual criminal charges, is the solidification of an image and a subsequent celebration of that image, which is bolstered by any demonstration of this activity in real life. The hyperreal creates a media image that directs attention away from the actual occurrences and thus puts us in the realm of pure spectacle.

To focus on the "real" alone misses the point. We are encouraged to read beyond the literal. Our focus must be on the hyperreal, or as Guy Debord says, in contemporary society "everything that was directly lived has moved away into a representation" (1). In other words, there is no real other than that which has been represented through imagery. In the collusion between image and reality in gangsta rap, we must begin to approximate the significance of what is configured as the ultramasculine identity of Dre, Tupac, or Snoop through representation, as opposed to arguing about the relative morality of social actions. Otherwise, we simply become moral arbitrators, as opposed to critics who can acknowledge these moral concerns, but do so in a way that can explicate the subtlest nuances of cultural production.

The multi-mediated context in which gangsta rap exists, combined with the discourse of the hyperreal, circulates throughout much of American popular culture and makes this investigation useful. In relation to larger cultural issues, one need only notice the popularity of daytime talk shows and their reliance on personal narratives that veer toward the grotesque and the perverse. The more sensational the story, the more likely that it will be presented as a kind of televisual autobiography.

In terms of prime-time broadcasting, the news magazine format offers a vehicle for a certain truthfulness in comparison to the fictional nature of most programming. These shows are extensions of this hyperreal phenomenon. The fact that their content is supposedly nonfiction separates them from most other forms of prime-time network television. But, as demonstrated by the highly publicized situation between NBC and General Motors over the network's rigging of an explosive to visually substantiate a point about exploding vehicles, we can never be sure whether we are experiencing the real or the imaginary. Thus we are in a constant state of the hyperreal once again.

This circulation of the hyperreal aesthetic operates both in mainstream society and in the cloistered world of gangsta culture. As author Brian Cross explains, "for new generations the culture produced by the seeming hopelessness of the gangsta lifestyle has become the social realism of the nineties" (32). With one of the most popular images of Black masculinity being the gangsta, it is necessary to unravel this complex scenario in order to understand the simultaneous infatuation and repulsion that has characterized the public's response to this cultural movement.

Way Out West

As rap music gained public momentum during the late 1980s, it was still a primarily East Coast movement, centered in New York City. Yet as the music began to evolve from a vehicle for male posturing into a discursive arena which foregrounded political concerns, it also began to slowly move away from its New York base into other areas of the country, most notably Los Angeles and the West Coast.[3]

In the early 1950s, a number of white jazz musicians emerged on the West Coast playing music which was radically different from what had become the rage of New York, bebop. The popularization of the "cool" sound on the West Coast, patterned on the innovations of Miles Davis's 1949 album (released in 1953), *The Birth of the Cool*, was a rejection of East Coast jazz as a truly Black idiom of expression. Instead, West Coast jazz attempted to create a space for white articulation without the burden of having to deal with the "Blackness" of what had become jazz's dominant discourse. The geographical distinction between New York, especially Harlem, and Los Angeles is instructive in understanding the vast difference between the music being played on the two coasts. The West Coast was indeed regarded as a "white" space of opposition.

Rap underwent a similar move westward in the late 1980s. As the West Coast became a popular image throughout the 1980s as a postmodern alternative to the East Coast, especially in terms of technology and culture, it was inevitable that a different and distinctly West Coast African American voice would emerge in the process. One of the early underground hits of the gangsta rap movement, "Boyz n the Hood," from which John Singleton drew the name of his first film, was originally written to be performed by the East Coast rap group HBO. According to Dr. Dre, the song's producer, HBO rejected the tune on the basis of its being "some west coast shit" (Cross, 187).

Whereas the shift westward in jazz indicated a racial dichotomy between black and white styles and musicians, the split between east and west in rap signified an internal dynamic within African American culture. This argument can be extended to gang culture itself. According to Monster Kody, "today, Crips are the number one killers of Crips" (19). This internal war of the Crips, or "set trippin'" as it is referred to, suggests the impact of violence among people who are united by gang affiliation, who supposedly have something in common; thus the popular media phrase "black-on-black" crime. In the same way that set trippin' locates conflict internally, we can see the dynamic of differences between East and West Coast notions of Blackness.

This internal split is clearly exemplified in East Coast rapper Tim Dog's assertive title "Fuck Compton" and Rodney-O and Joe Cooley's response, "Fuck New York." In both cases the identification of urban space is instrumental in defining identity. The specifically internal definition serves as a rejection of the often unifying metaphor of race.

This shift to the West Coast in rap allowed for the articulation of a geographical specificity which was considered unique and "authentic" to one's experiences in the gang-dominated culture of South Central Los Angeles. The move to the West Coast and the subsequent emergence of gangsta rap openly critique the way that race is often treated monolithically by the mainstream media.[4]

This music was an assertion of individuality, and what better way to articulate individual experiences than to detail events in one's immediate environment or "'hood"? What could be more individualized, and in turn argued for as authentic, than the personal experiences of one's own communal existence? According to Tricia Rose, "identity in hip-hop communities is deeply rooted in the specific, the local experience, and one's attachment to and status in a local group or alternative family" (Black Noise, 34).

Thus, the specific neighborhood or set, often encompassing a geographical area as small as an individual street—e.g., the Eight Trey

Gangsta Crips represent 83rd street between Florence and Normandie—became the locus of identity that distinguished various factions within gangsta culture. Boundaries, both real and imaginary, signaled the importance of space and signified a politics of location that sees the acquisition of space as fundamental to identity formation.

Public Enemy's 1988 release, *It Takes a Nation of Millions to Hold Us Back*, a record often thought of as the canonical text for political rap, was gaining mainstream popularity at the same time that NWA's second release, *Straight outta Compton*, was being targeted by the FBI as encouraging the murder of police. Though Public Enemy's album is about the popularizing of political culture, NWA's is about the state's acknowledgment of what it sees as the threatening iconography of gangsta culture. As rap was establishing itself as a vehicle for political expression, it was also showing early signs of the move away from this East Coast–based agenda and at the same time solidifying its cultural position. Letters of reprimand from the FBI worked to strengthen a notorious identity, as opposed to removing it from the cultural landscape.

Like the quintessential "bad nigga" of African American folklore, the gangsta rapper would come to be simultaneously celebrated and feared, both by the outside world and by those in the community. When Ice Cube boldly proclaims himself "the bitch killer/cop killer" in "The Nigga You Love to Hate," it is obvious that he sees oppression by the police as equally repulsive as the presence of women, especially Black women. Gangsta rappers, like the bad nigga, find community only among themselves, and even that bond is constantly being challenged.

Thus, in 1988 as the political edge of rap was taking hold in the popular imagination, opening up discussions surrounding a resurgent Black nationalism and ideas of Afrocentricity, gangsta rap was emerging as a defiant form which not only would threaten those on the outside, here represented by an overzealous FBI, but eventually would become the antithesis of any sustained political discourse in popular culture. In this sense, gangsta rap is, in many ways, about the death of political discourse in African American popular culture.

The Revolutionary Lumpenproletariat

Yet there is a link between politics and "gangsterism" that cannot be avoided. As Mike Davis has argued in his provocative *City of Quartz*, the original Crips were an offshoot of the Black Panther Party. Davis, who consistently references Donald Bakeer, the author of *South Central*, the book from which the Steve Anderson film of the same name was adapted, states that the original acronym CRIP stood for "Community Revolution in Progress" (299). Davis goes on to say that the Crips "inherited the Panther aura of fearlessness and transmitted the ideology of armed vanguardism (short of its program)."

According to Elaine Brown in her autobiography and revisionist history of the Panthers, *A Taste of Power*, many members of the party were themselves gangsters at one time. This, coupled with the legend of Malcolm X's life in the gangster underworld prior to his joining the Nation of Islam, indicates that Black gangsters have always made an easy transition to a position in the political vanguard. This tendency represents what Davis has called "the revolutionary lumpenproletariat."

Most representative of this transition from gangster to political ideologue is West Coast rapper Ice Cube. Originally a founding member of NWA, Ice Cube was the primary writer for most of their early material, most notably "Fuck tha Police." His departure from the group in 1989 was an important event in the history of rap music. If NWA's *Straight outta Compton* is the record that brought nationwide attention to the developing genre of gangsta rap, then Ice Cube's first solo effort, *Amerikkka's Most Wanted* (1990), demonstrated that this music was going to be more than a passing trend. Its release also began the cultural process that would make Ice Cube one of the few rap superstars.

Ice Cube underwent a rapid evolution in his musical life from his days as the lyricist for NWA to his prominent position only a few short years later. Many rap acts have been popular on a single or maybe an album, but very few have a body of work that includes five albums: an extended-play (EP) record, *Kill at Will*; lead production credits on three YoYo records—*Make Room for the Motherlode* (1991), *Black Pearl* (1992), and *You Better Ask Somebody* (1993)—and Mack 10's debut release, *Foe Life* (1995); an extremely popular Da Lench Mob album, *Guerrillas in the Mist* (1992); not to mention his early work with NWA.

In a music industry replete with "one-hit wonders," Ice Cube's continued success is a mark of the transition of gangsta rap from marginal to mainstream—a transition that he had a great deal to do with. Ice Cube even alludes to this on his 1992 album *The Predator* when he asks the self-reflexively rhetorical question, "Nigga wit the third album, how come you don't fall off?"

The transition from pure gangster to ideological gangster is not a simple one. The first solo record, *Amerikkka's Most Wanted*, demonstrates the narrative qualities that distinguish Ice Cube from all competitors. This album is a first-person account of the trials and tribulations of living in South Central L.A. His storytelling ability is truly in the same league as that of a Richard Wright or Ralph Ellison, adapted to the modern medium of rap music and contemporary society. With as much detail as one can convey lyrically, Ice Cube forces his familiarity of the "'hood" on the listener in such an effective way that areas of South Central become as common a public Southern California landmark as Rodeo Drive or the ubiquitous Hollywood sign.

The album opens with Ice Cube being marched to the electric chair. When asked if he has any last words, he responds, "Yeah, I got some last words, fuck all y'all," at which point we hear a loud "switch" indicating that he has now been executed. Immediately following this execution, he goes on to castigate a number of aspects of American society in the provocatively titled "The Nigga You Love to Hate." His targets include sell-out rappers, mainstream African American celebrities, police, women in general, and anyone else who happens to get in his way.

One of the most notable lines on the record contains a quick deconstruction of the escalating fame of late-night talk show host Arsenio Hall: "They ask me if I liked Arsenio / 'Bout as much as the bicentennial." He also expresses his open contempt for the mainstream. His rejection of mainstream society would parallel many of the opening solos performed by John Coltrane during the latter part of his musical life. Ice Cube has repeated this opening strategy on all of his ensuing projects.

While this first album clearly establishes Ice Cube's utter defiance of white racism and African American complicity, it would be the one and only album of its kind from him. *Amerikkka's Most Wanted* represents the perfect distillation of gangsta culture, a nihilistic celebration of the aggressive excesses of Black male ghetto life presented in its most sensationalistic fashion, without apologies or misgivings. Whereas this record, like *Straight outta Compton* before it, is a detailed cruise through the mind of a young "G," his next album, *Death Certificate* (1991), took a much more politicized stance, while remaining true to its gangsta rap roots.

On the album cover of *Death Certificate*, we see an enthusiastic Ice Cube with his right hand placed firmly over his heart in mock reverence, standing over a dead body which lies on a gurney. The body is wrapped in the American flag, and the toe tag identifies it as that of "Uncle Sam." The metaphoric death of "America" and all that it stands for clearly indicates that a more political direction is intended on this record. Ice Cube furthers this theme on the tune "I Wanna Kill Sam," in which he declares, "I wanna kill Sam / Cause he ain't my muthafucking uncle." *Death Certificate* suggests Ice Cube's coming to consciousness in the gangster-to-revolutionary tradition of both Malcolm X and the Black Panther Party.

In addition to being a concept album, akin to Marvin Gaye's *What's Going On* (1971), the record is divided into the "Death" and the "Life" sides. Ice Cube begins the album with the following proclamation: "Niggaz are a state of emergency / The death side / A mirrored image of where we are today / The life side / A vision of where we need to go / So sign your death certificate."

The Death side is a continuation of *Amerikkka's Most Wanted* in that it chronicles the devastation and social ills of the ghetto landscape of South Central L.A. The topics range from sexually promiscuous women ("Giving Up the Nappy Dugout"), the rampancy of sexually transmitted disease ("Look Who's Burning"), the constant need to be armed or "strapped" in the volatile ghetto ("Man's Best Friend"), and the exportation of gang and drug culture to the Midwest and other areas of the country ("My Summer Vacation"). Yet it is the Life side that takes this album to another level. The Life side contains a series of societal critiques that deal with, among other things, white male stereotyping and the sexual harassment of Black women ("Horny Lil Devil"), selling out in general ("True to the Game"), the constant danger of gang life ("Color Blind"), and a self-reflexive critique of Black people's own participation in their oppression ("Us"). This side also includes a controversial track entitled "Black Korea" which anticipates the African American vs. Korean American conflicts that began to receive widespread media attention in the aftermath of the L.A. uprising in April 1992.

The most important thing about this side is the influence that the teachings of the Nation of Islam have had on Ice Cube's thinking. With several references to the language and icons of the Nation, Ice Cube's political position stands out. It is clear that he has become an advocate of a historically ideological position, but nuances this ideology in a fashion specific to the genre within which he exists. This fusion of gangsta iconography and Nation of Islam theology is clearly indicated in the photo insert contained inside the compact disc packaging.

First of all there is a noticeable difference in his appearance from the first album, where we see Ice Cube dressed all in black, wearing a skullcap with the ends of his jheri curl peeping out from the rear. He is standing in front of several similarly clad members of his crew in L.A.'s historic garment district. On the cover of his second album, Ice Cube has shaved his head, cutting off his infamous jheri curl, a hairstyle that had long since faded from popularity everywhere but in South Central Los Angeles. This defiance of accepted style had been his trademark on the first album and was the trademark of many L.A. gang members as well. Yet on *Death Certificate* he openly rejects this style altogether: "Cut that jheri juice / And get a bald head / Then let it nap up." Ice Cube's rejection of this chemically treated hairstyle, similar to Malcolm X's rejection of his "konk," is no longer considered consistent with his changing image and his coming to Black consciousness, while the bald-headed African American male, from boxer Jack Johnson forward, has always connoted virile masculinity. The bald head had at the time of this album once again become a popular style among African American males, especially athletes and rappers. His reference to letting it "nap up" further signifies his recognition of a Black aesthetic and his refusal to accept dominant standards of beauty.

In addition to this new appearance, we see Ice Cube reading from *The Final Call*, the Nation of Islam's bi-weekly newspaper. He is in the middle of the picture, with the image divided into two groups on either side of him. On one side we see several members of Ice Cube's "posse," Da Lench Mob, dressed in various phases of "G" style. On the other side we see several suit- and bow-tie-wearing members of the Fruit of Islam, the security force for the Nation. As the headline on *The Final Call* reads "UNITE or PERISH," Ice Cube's presence symbolically attempts to unify these two separate groups.

This visual unification underscores the thematic unity of the album itself. The coupling of gangsta iconography with the Nation's specific brand of Black nationalism would eventually define Ice Cube's image. Like the Black Panther Party, Ice Cube was a gangster who had come to a specific political consciousness from his location on the ghetto streets. Yet in the same way as the Panthers, especially in light of Elaine Brown's revisionism, he remains a part of his original gangsta community nonetheless. Oscillating between the two poles of identity would distinguish Ice Cube as both a rapper and a popular Black male icon. It is impossible to deny Ice Cube's impact on the genre, but it is also important to point out that his significance in crossing the boundaries between gangsta and ideologue is not shared by other rappers.

What has happened with L.A. gang culture, after the FBI and LAPD's concerted effort to annihilate any form of empowered political articulation from the community, is a reversal of the previous transition from gangster to revolutionary. Instead we have seen the one-time revolutionaries accept the violent tropes of political resistance without the informed ideology that separates gangsters from freedom fighters. In a similar fashion, the move from the politicized domain of East Coast rap championed by Public Enemy to the celebratory nihilism of West Coast gangsta rap demonstrates the current death of acknowledged political activism in contemporary culture.

Ain't Nothing But a "G" Thang

This political decline is also consistent with the position advocated by Dr. Dre. In an interview with Brian Cross when discussing his entrance into gangsta rap as a producer, Dre says, "I wanted to go all the way left, everybody trying to do this black power and shit, I was like let's give 'em an alternative" (197). It is interesting that the alternative comes in the form of celebrating the antithesis of politics through gangsta rap. He goes on to say, in reference to the purpose and function of making records, "It ain't about who's the hardest, it's about who makes the best record, as a matter of fact it ain't even about that, it's about who sells the most records" (197).

These open statements, which both denounce politics and in some way denounce the celebration of craft for the primary objective of making money, are creatively incorporated into his music in "Dre Day," in which Dre emphatically announces, "No medallions / Dreadlocks / Or Black fist / It's just that gangsta glare / With gangsta rap / That gangsta shit / Brings a gang of snaps." These obvious symbols of Black nationalism are rejected in favor of celebrating capital (snaps), excess, grotesque spectacle, and the nihilism that pervades gangsta culture. Dr. Dre's attitude toward the function of rap in the music business and his attitude toward Black nationalism in general clearly state the politics of an antipolitical movement.

This eager embrace of the excesses of capitalism places Dre and his contemporaries in the company of arch-conservative proponents of a free-market economy. This argument is supported by deceased AIDS victim Easy E and his much-discussed appearance at a Republican Party fundraiser in 1991. Yet as Easy himself asked rhetorically, How can someone make a song like "Fuck tha Police" and be a Republican? This reductionistic reading is ultimately too simplistic to accommodate the contradictions of this approach. It would be more interesting to locate Dre's position, like that of the underworld gangsta, on the axis of a capitalist metacritique, which sees the manipulation of capitalism by African Americans, in terms of both art and business practices, as a perverse deconstruction of a monopoly enjoyed primarily by white male corporate interests.

Dre's rise to prominence in the world of gangsta rap highlights the salient qualities of this cultural movement. Thematically, Dre's style features the glamorization of wanton violence, a propensity toward self-indulgence, and the exaggeration of these forms through the use of spectacle. This reliance on spectacle is demonstrated most clearly in the overall production values of the work, especially as it relates to an overt theatricality. *The Chronic* features a number of pieces of comedic dialogue, many of which openly reinscribe the marginal position of women in this world, as well as the re-creation of episodes of popular culture, adapted to the gangsta idiom. In the "$20 Sack Pyramid," a group of contestants, in the style of a popular game show, compete for a bag of marijuana and a trip to the Compton swap meet. This type of comedic skit is combined with the use of special sound effects and themes of violence. It also draws on the music of George Clinton, which works to define Dr. Dre's popularity. He has tapped into several illuminating areas of popular culture in a way reminiscent of the voyeuristic pleasure associated with the films of Quentin Tarantino, which have taken pop trivia to its most extreme form. Once again excess and the pushing of the boundaries of "acceptable" taste have come to augment much of what now exists throughout the cultural landscape.

Dre has taken the production end of rap into an entirely new and different arena, for once making production somewhat superior to the lyrical styling of the rappers themselves. The production values for both Dr. Dre's record *The Chronic* and his partner Snoop Doggy Dogg's *Doggystyle* are similar, firmly rooted in Dre's landmark "g funk" style, which uses the imagery of the "g" in conjunction with funk-inspired beats of the 1970s, especially those of George Clinton. This combination helped to make the "g funk era" popular on a mass scale.

Both Dre and Snoop realize the importance of video in promoting records, as each of their music videos provides a slice of lower-class Black life in South Central and Long Beach. When MTV began listing the directors' names during the playing of music videos, this recent form of popular culture took on cinematic overtones, giving individuals such as Dr. Dre the opportunity to create their own visual images to accompany the illuminating lyrics that had been the defining component of the music.

Thus in the very popular video to "Ain't Nothing But a 'G' Thang," we witness Dre's directorial skills along with his noted musical production. Dre has used the video format to articulate the nuances of ghetto life in a seemingly authentic fashion. For instance, "G Thang" takes us on an ethnographic excursion into the "'hood" by highlighting such things as a barren front lawn, a gun tucked neatly into the small of someone's back, a refrigerator full of Olde English Malt Liquor, and a festive community picnic as Snoop and Dre ride through South Central in their low riders. In a similar fashion, "Let Me Ride" features various local landmarks, such as a popular hand car wash, frequented by several "ballers," in the Crenshaw District as well as other areas throughout South Central.

The localizing effect allows Dre to clearly link himself with the community that is so vital to his musical authenticity. This link also provides a specialized view of Los Angeles quite different from that conveyed through other forms of popular representation. The ability to explicate the nuances of a local community and forge this explication with musical distinction results in something akin to an ethnographer's oral history, yet in this case the ethnographer is part of the very community that he attempts to represent. Dre's use of the video medium, and his subsequent direction of the short film *Murder Was the Case* (1994), demonstrate how gangsta rap has merged with the visual means of production to provide an alternate voice in light of the film industry's hesitancy regarding a full-fledged development of Black cinema. As the foundation for this excursion into pop culture at a larger level, music has once again been the motivating factor behind advances in other areas of culture. The fact that these new ventures are specific to a racialized reading of Los Angeles in the postindustrial era makes the situation that much more illuminating in regard to the representation of race, class, and Black masculinity in contemporary urban America.

Gangsta rap paints a vivid picture of the identity politics of Black masculinity in Los Angeles. While the tendency has been to criticize this music for its celebration of violence and misogyny and its nihilistic approach to life, it is important to understand the cultural currents that shape the thematic content.

Gangsta culture mirrors other forms while retaining its distinctiveness. It is clearly influenced by the extreme spectacle of Hollywood; the metaphoric closeness between the industry and the various 'hoods of Los Angeles cannot be denied. Gangsta culture is clearly informed by the visual, and the images that circulate through the lyrics of the music lend themselves easily to the production of visual culture, as Dr. Dre's direction of *Murder Was the Case*, which is based on a Snoop Doggy Dogg song, indicates.

While Dr. Dre and Ice Cube's collaboration *Natural Born Killers* (1994) takes its cue from Oliver Stone's film of the same name, they put their own spin on the culture's obsession with violence. In both cases, simple-minded perceptions inform the logic that these acts encourage the pathology, but we should look at the entire cultural context, specifically the full spectrum of gangsta culture, its exposition on lower-class Black masculinity, and its placement in contemporary Los Angeles. Thus a full exposition of the culture is paramount to understanding the relevant issues within a form that is either neglected or misread by a limiting moral critique.

Young, Black, and Don't Give a Fuck: Experiencing the Cinema of Nihilism

I'm larger than that nigga Steven Segal.

—O Dog, *Menace II Society*

Although the contemporary expression of the gangsta is primarily a result of the thematics of gangsta rap, a concurrent episode has taken place in the world of Black film. With the resurgence of African American cinema in the late 1980s and the 1990s, there has been a lot of emphasis placed on the life of the gangsta from a cinematic standpoint. Clearly some of the most profitable films—e.g., *New Jack City*, *Boyz n the Hood*, and *Juice*—of the newest wave of African American cinema have been related in some way to the gangsta genre.

This chapter will explore how this genre has resurfaced in film, with specific attention to the history of the gangster genre, both in a larger sense and in relation to the Blaxploitation era. In addition to looking at the influences of gangster films on the contemporary gangsta film, we will look to place this recent revisitation in the context of the discourse of postindustrial Black Los Angeles.

Thus our focus will be on two films as competing versions of the gangsta narrative, John Singleton's *Boyz n the Hood* and Allen and Albert Hughes's *Menace II Society.* As both a point of critique and a furthering of the context of race in 1990s Los Angeles, the chapter will also look at Edward James Olmos's *American Me*, a gangsta film which focuses on Latinos, in contrast to the previously mentioned films, which deal exclusively with African Americans. Given that Latino culture is vital to understanding Los Angeles, especially its working- and lower-class sectors, the analysis of *American Me* will substantiate the understanding of the gangsta.

So You Wanna Be a Gangsta?

The gangster film and the Western are two of the most important genres in the history of Hollywood, especially with respect to articulation of the discourse of American history and masculinity. Whereas the western concentrated on the mythic settling of the West and a perceived notion of progression, it was primarily concerned with the frontier mentality of the eighteenth through the late nineteenth century. The gangster genre, on the other hand, is about the evolution of American society in the twentieth century into a legitimate entity in the world economy.

Though the western covertly articulated the politics of oppression against Native Americans during the settling of the West, the gangster genre focused on questions of ethnicity—e.g., Italian, Irish—and how these are transformed over time into questions of race—Black, Latino, etc. This ideological shift provided an interesting representation of the significant position that race has come to occupy in the discourse of American society. We must look at the transformation of the linguistic sign "gangster" and its slow transition to its most recent embodiment as "gangsta" as an instructive historical metaphor.

The respelling of the word "gangster" is key to understanding the current function of this particular movement. The transition from "gangster" to "gangsta" is quite illuminating with respect to the accompanying historical, racial, and societal changes.

Americans have always had a fascination with the underworld society populated by those who openly resisted the laws of dominant society and instead created their own world, living by their own rules. Gangsters have in many ways been our version of revolutionaries throughout history. Whereas Europe has always had real-life political revolutionaries, twentieth-century American discourse, upheld by police and government activity, seems to have found ways of perverting for the public the political voices that exist outside the narrow traditions of allowed political expression.

The displacement of these political voices by the forces of oppression has created a renegade space within American culture that allows for the expression of gangster culture. Gangsters indeed function as somewhat revolutionary in comparison to the rest of society, as demonstrated by their open defiance of accepted societal norms and laws, existence in their own environment, and circulation of their own alternative capital. This allows them to remain part of the larger society but to fully exist in their own communities at the same time. This lifestyle has been a consistent media staple throughout the twentieth century, particularly in film.

From as early as D. W. Griffith's *Musketeers of Pig Alley* (1912) and the celebrated studio films of the 1930s—e.g., *Little Caesar* (1930), *Public Enemy* (1931), and *Scarface* (1932)—through the epic treatment rendered in the first two *Godfather* films (1972, 1974), the gangster has enjoyed a vivid screen life. What is important here is that these criminals, as they are deemed by the dominant society, are defined as deviant primarily because of issues of ethnicity, as opposed to issues of race, though to some extent all definitions of ethnicity in this context are inevitably influenced by a subtle definition of race.

This emphasis on ethnicity as it functions in opposition to the standard "white Anglo-Saxon Protestant" is summarized in the first two *Godfather* films. As the United States, both at and immediately after the turn of the century, increasingly became a nation of European immigrants, incoming Italians were consigned to the bottom of the social ladder. In the opening segment of *Godfather II*, Michael Corleone is berated and verbally abused by Senator Geery of Nevada because of his Italian heritage. The word "Italian" is set in opposition to "American" constantly in this segment so as to highlight the ethnic hierarchy which remains a foundational issue in this film. Corleone's ascension to power is complicated by his inability to fully surmount this societal obstacle, at least at this point in the film, and by extension that point in American history—the early 1950s.

It is Francis Ford Coppola's argument that such oppression forced these Italian immigrants into a subversive lifestyle and economy much like that practiced throughout southern Italy, especially in Sicily. Borrowing from their own cultural tradition, some of these new Americans used the underground economy as a vital means of sustenance in the face of ethnic, religious, and cultural oppression. And though their desire, being heavily influenced by the discourse of an "American dream," was to ultimately be fully assimilated into American society, the achievement of this desire was revealed to be at the cost of losing their ethnic and cultural heritage.

Ultimately, the *Godfather* films are about how American society forced those turn-of-the-century immigrants to reject their own culturally distinctive voices in favor of a uniquely "American" voice, one that was homogeneous as opposed to being heterogeneous. Yet these films are distinguished from numerous others that have tried to tell the same story by the argument that American culture at some point willingly integrated the excesses of ethnically defined gangster culture, especially from an economic standpoint, into the structure of larger American society. Thus the political economy of America is indebted at some level to the exploits of gangster culture.

This thesis is in direct opposition to the usual fundamentally conservative ideology regarding the foundations of twentieth-century American society. Therefore, the *Godfather* films are a brilliant example of a Marxist-influenced revisionist history, functioning as an astute treatise on ethnicity, assimilation, and the relevance of political economy to the understanding of twentieth-century American history. By the conclusion of *Godfather II*, Michael Corleone is indistinguishable from the America that surrounds him. As indicated by the murder of his brother, Frado, he has been completely assimilated into the narrative fabric of American society. By putting the interests of capitalism over family and culture, Michael has cut off all links to his immigrant heritage and has thereby been admitted to the corridors of power that define elite American society.

At a larger level, the film's historical themes indicate the assimilation of ethnicity into a homogeneous American society, yet foreground the continued rejection of race as a component of the metaphoric "melting pot"—because it is the challenge of race that accelerates the assimilative process of ethnicity.

In the first *Godfather* film, we see this same social dynamic at play regarding ethnicity over race. Near the film's conclusion, we witness the memorable meeting of the "heads of the five families," where the dilemmas of drug trafficking are being discussed by the various Mafia leaders. Vito Corleone is characterized as opposing this potentially lucrative venture for moral reasons, while many of the other members are excited about the possible financial benefits. The chieftain from Kansas City suggests that the Mafia should engage in selling drugs, but only at a distance, leaving the underside of this environment to be experienced by what he describes as the "dark people" because, as he adds, "they're animals anyway, let them lose their souls." His use of the phrase "dark people" and his labeling of them as "animals" clearly reference African Americans, and by extension racialized others in general. This line of dialogue is viewed by many African Americans as prophetic, seeing that the release of *The Godfather* in the early 1970s closely paralleled the upsurge in underworld drug activity throughout African American ghetto communities.

In relation to the assimilation of ethnicity at the expense of race, this line also signifies the way in which the previously mentioned structural hierarchy exists aside from the racial hierarchy, which many African Americans have been unable to transcend because of the difference in skin color. Though Italians through this perverted formulation could be considered inferior to "wasps," those traits that make them different can be easily subsumed when contrasted with the obvious difference of skin color and the history that goes along with being darker. It is in this context that the thematic progression of the *Godfather* films signals the end of the public fascination with the Italian gangster and his ethnically rich underworld.

Furthermore, this line indicates that the drug culture would be an important turning point in the historical discourse specific to the question of race as time moved forward. This line of reasoning has been pursued in numerous texts, most recently through Bill Duke's film *Deep Cover* (1992), which comments on the conspiracy involved in both furnishing and addicting segments of the Black community with drugs as a political maneuver by the government to keep these individuals sedated and oppressed so as to quell any potential political resistance. Mario Van Peebles's film *Panther* (1995) asserts the same theory in connection with the attempted destruction of the Black Panther Party by J. Edgar Hoover and the FBI. In both cases, crime can be seen as affirming capitalism, yet in specifically racial terms.

With this assimilation of ethnicity as signified through the Coppola films, America finds the need to fulfill this otherwise empty space with the next logical descending step on the social ladder, that being race.[1] Two other films from the 1980s effectively mark the shift away from the ethnic gangster to the racialized gangsta. Brian De Palma's remake of *Scarface* (1983) is an obvious rewriting of the genre from the perspective of race. Whereas the main character in the 1932 film was an Italian, in the De Palma version we deal with a racialized Cuban.

Drawing from real political events, De Palma's film begins with the Mariel boat lift of Cuban refugees into south Florida during the latter part of the 1970s, an event which many still consider a lingering legacy of Jimmy Carter's presidency. The film's main character, Tony Montana, is clearly foregrounded as a racialized other. His Cuban identity, broken accent, penchant for garishness, and overall ruthless approach to wealth and human life served as the basis for the popular media representation of Latin American drug dealers that came to dominate the 1980s.

With an increase in drug paranoia from the conservative Reagan and Bush administrations, this form of representation would nearly erase past images of Italian mob figures from the popular memory. While John Gotti was a celebrated folk hero for his stylish media-friendly disposition, individuals such as Carlos Lader Rivas, Pablo Escobar, and Manuel Noriega, who became common sights on the evening news and network news magazine programs, were depicted as threats to the very fabric of our society. To add to this popular form of representation, NBC's series *Miami Vice* drew many of its story lines and criminal figures from this newly accepted version of racialized representation.[2]

The De Palma film was an overblown attempt to detail the rise and fall of a modern-day criminal, redefining the gangster tradition along the way. While it summarized the aggressive accumulation of capital so typical of 1980s culture, the impact of the text on contemporary society lay in the iconic viability of the main character. The Latin American drug dealer, as epitomized by Al Pacino's character in *Scarface*, would occupy a central place in a criminal culture that would become increasingly defined by race during these politically conservative years.

The other major filmic event that reflected this obsession with the drug culture and the question of race was Dennis Hopper's *Colors* (1988). Hopper's film offered an intricate look at the gang culture that existed in both South Central and East Los Angeles. Its main characters were two white Los Angeles police officers who were commissioned with the monumental task of eliminating the urban crime being perpetrated by African American and Latino youth. This film tied in neatly with the increasing commentary presented by national news programs about what had begun as a regional situation and was later argued to have spread throughout the country. Using the police, and by extension the rest of white society, as its victims, the film endorsed the racial paranoia concerning criminality that at this time was in full swing.

Colors, for all intents and purposes, made the gangbanger America's contemporary criminal of choice, turning a localized problem into a national epidemic that once again linked crime with specific notions of race. In many ways, *Colors* served the same function for gangsta culture that *Birth of a Nation* served for the early stages of African American cinema. Both films, through their overt racial paranoia, and in both cases using armed militia as an answer to the perceived Black threat— in one case the Ku Klux Klan, in the other a racist police department— inspired a series of African American cinematic responses. This regressive film engendered a public fascination with the newly defined "gangsta."

With the traditional white ethnic gangster film having all but disappeared, the way was clear for the entrance of a new popular villain to be screened across the mind of American society. The ideological link between crime and race would be made worse, and the image of the African American gangbanger would become not only popular in the sense of repeated representation, but financially lucrative as well. In addition to the changing history of the Hollywood gangster film, several other historical factors specific to African American culture would contribute to the emergence and eventual proliferation of the African American "gangsta."

From the Black Godfather
to the Black Guerrilla Family

The late 1960s and early 1970s saw an increase in underworld activity, especially involving drugs, throughout many lower-class Black communities. In many ways more important than the drugs themselves was the culture that accompanied this underworld lifestyle and the way in which it was represented visually. The garish fashions popularized by Eleganza and Flag Brothers, heavily adorned, ornament-laden Cadillacs, and other materialistic excesses helped to define this cultural terrain as "cool" during this period.

These issues are interestingly summed up in the popular 1973 song by William DeVaugh, "Be Thankful for What You've Got," with its refrain "Diamond in the back / Sunroof top / Diggin' in the seam / With the gangster lean." Though DeVaugh's song was intended as a critique of this lifestyle, as the tune encourages the listener not to be obsessed with these material possessions—"You may not have a car at all / But remember brothers and sisters / You can still stand tall"—the lyrics about gangster style take precedence.

The Black gangster was celebrated throughout popular culture as well as in several sectors of lower-class society, in much the same way that Coppola's films glamorize the underworld that they try to criticize. The strength of the critique is often lost, misread, or compromised because of the vivid visual detail used to depict "the life." Though I would disagree with harsh, though popular, critical assessments such as that of Ed Guerrero, who summarizes the effects of this phenomenon as "the cinematic inscription and glorification of the parasitic, hustling milieu of the black urban underworld" (96), there is clearly a discrepancy between the political messages being articulated and popular audience reception.

In several of the films that define this period, eventually known as the "Blaxploitation" era of Hollywood (1970–73), the Black protagonist was presented in opposition to a stereotypical white menace who was bent on destroying the African American community, primarily through the influx of drugs and the accompanying culture of violence. For the most part, evil in the films was personified in the form of a corrupt police or mafia figure, if not both at the same time. Thus much of the narrative action appeared in battles between some faction of the white mafia, who had traditionally been in control of the ghetto, albeit from a distance, and the emerging Black underworld figures who were striving to wrest control of this alternative economy from their white counterparts.

It was as if the loosening of societal restrictions gained during the civil rights movement permitted exploitation of the community through control of underworld vices, though the actual control was in the hands of manipulative outsiders, who used the Black gangster as their foil. The Black gangster, whether he was a pimp, dope dealer, or hustler, through these films became a prominent example of what it meant to be an entrepreneur. The tension between outside influence and inside control is represented in many of the films of the period, most notably *Cotton Comes to Harlem*, *Across 110th Street*, *Superfly*, and *The Mack*. The African American gangster had become a media staple by the mid-1970s.

Gordon Parks Jr.'s ghetto masterpiece *Superfly* (1972) opens with a high-angle crane shot which frames two enterprising heroin addicts in the process of devising a scheme that will momentarily mollify their collective "jones." As the camera descends, the tune on the soundtrack, Curtis Mayfield's "Little Child Running Wild," becomes increasingly prominent. The juxtaposition of sound and image here reveals ghetto existence to be one of resistant complicity. Instead of simply foregrounding the perils of drug addiction, the scene offers the insightful analysis of Mayfield's lyrics: "Little child / Running wild / Watch a while / To see he never smiles / Broken home / Father gone / Mama tired / His soul is all alone."

This opening sets up the struggle that characterizes the remainder of the film, and by extension the plight of African Americans in general. Faced with dismal opportunities for advancement in a racist society, the film's main character, the stylish Youngblood Priest, actively participates in "the life," as the underworld environment of hustling is colloquially referred to. In one of the film's early pivotal scenes, as Priest attempts to inform his partner, Eddie, of his plan to leave the dope game after one last score, Eddie resists, suggesting that Priest cherish his elite material status. The seductive "freedom" associated with capitalism is epitomized in Eddie's next line, when he informs Priest that he currently enjoys "a color TV in every room, an eight-track stereo, and can snort a half a piece a dope a day." Eddie defines this life of luxury as "the American Dream, nigga," the word "nigga" here emphasizing Priest's realization of the "dream" in a particularly "Black" form. In conclusion, Eddie persuades Priest by suggesting that he "better come on in."

Eddie's encouragement demonstrates his full acceptance of materialism at the expense of his own existential freedom. His embrace of capitalism is seen as a logical response to being an oppressed member of a marginalized group. This substitution of materialism for self-esteem is further underscored by Curtis Mayfield's penetrating tune "Eddie You Should Have Known Better" on the film's soundtrack. As Mayfield alludes, "Eddie you should have known better / Brother you know you wrong / Think of the tears and fears you bring to your folks back home." Eddie has truly "sold out," and this has even larger implications for African American culture. Though one may enjoy the material benefits of individual assimilation, these pleasures are at the expense of the overall community.

Unlike his partner, Priest is dissatisfied with his societal entrapment and his lack of choices in life; thus he plans on leaving this lifestyle in search of an elusive notion of freedom. This is a true case of making the best of a bad situation, if not a modified version of the improvisation that lies at the core of African American oral expression. The film's conclusion offers a metaphorical illusion of freedom, as Priest not only insults the vile white police captain responsible for controlling the drug trade in the best of the Black signifying tradition, but he also walks away unharmed with all the money to boot. Hollywood would take this same formula, unquestioned Black triumph over evil white oppression, and replicate it endless numbers of times so as to turn the potentially revolutionary actions of African American cinema into a series of running gags, devoid of all political substance. As exemplified in Keenan Ivory Wayans's 1989 film *I'm Gonna Get You Sucka*, the Blaxploitation era became, for many, a comic reference point, and a regrettable debasement of the excesses of 1970s Black culture.

The Black "gangster," of which Priest is the epitome, became a central and prevalent image. Many of the films of this period were based on the dynamics of an African American underworld existence (e.g., *Sweetsweetback's Badass Song, The Mack, Willie Dynamite, Coffy, Cleopatra Jones*), and in conjunction with the popular ghetto literature of Iceberg Slim and Donald Goines, as well as the more esoteric works of author Chester Himes and playwright Charles Gordone, this form of representation remained viable long after this period had passed. In line with Nelson George's argument that "Blaxploitation movies are crucial to the current 70's retro-nuevo phase" (149), this historical period left a series of low-budget films which would eventually be perfect for transfer to the home video format. The "Blaxploitation" films would leave an indelible imprint on African American popular culture as the "gangsta" continued to rise in prominence and position.

A Small Introduction to the "G" Funk Era

With the historical antecedents of the Hollywood gangster film and 1970s Blaxploitation films, along with popular African American literature that explored the culture, the stage was set for the flowering of gangsta culture in the late 1980s and early 1990s. The contemporary manifestation continued to appear in the form of cinema, but also gained increasing visibility in the world of rap music, to the point of establishing its own genre and forming a solid cultural movement. This transition from genre to cultural movement included representations in film, music, and literature, and involved multiple layers of society: communal, political, and corporate. From the regular individuals whose personal narratives drew heavily from gangster culture, to rap artists whose real-life antics coincided with the fictional rhetoric of their lyrics, and finally to the highest levels of government, where questions of moral integrity, community debasement, and freedom of speech were constantly being posed, this cultural movement had a great deal of currency with respect to African Americans in society, especially the African American male.

The contribution of cinema to gangsta culture is indicative of the popularizing of the movement to a mainstream audience. Yet it is the exchange of imagery between cinema and rap music that defines this culture as more than simply a passing trend or an outdated genre. In essence, to talk about gangsta culture is to talk about gangsta rap. The music provides the themes and ethos of this particular cultural movement. To understand the transition of the music from an isolated subcultural phenomenon, played primarily in the various 'hoods of South Central Los Angeles, Compton, Long Beach, and Inglewood, to a mainstream media staple played out on MTV, is to understand the evolution from folk culture to popular culture—i.e., the blues—that has defined much of African American cultural production in the twentieth century.

Though there are glimpses of the gangster lifestyle in a number of films that appeared throughout the late 1980s and especially in the early 1990s, the two films most relevant to an understanding of gangsta culture are John Singleton's *Boyz n the Hood* (1991) and Allen and Albert Hughes's *Menace II Society* (1993). Not to ignore such a popular film as Mario Van Peebles's *New Jack City* (1991) or Abel Ferrera's cult video classic *The King of New York* (1990), but these texts are more directly influenced by the traditional gangster paradigm, in addition to being set in New York City. The filmic representation of gangsta culture draws many of its influences from rap music, and in turn rap music assumes a great deal of identity with the work of Singleton and the Hughes brothers. Contemporary gangsta culture is undoubtedly a West Coast phenomenon.

The other film that holds a vital position in the representation of gangsta culture is Edward James Olmos's *American Me* (1992). This film addresses the culture from a Latino perspective as opposed to an African American one. This is of utmost importance, for while gangsta culture is publicly regarded as an African American entity, much of the culture derives from the close proximity in which African Americans and Latinos coexist in racialized Los Angeles.

Thus the phenomenon of gangsta culture draws much of its thematic impetus from rap music, articulates itself in the contested spaces of South Central Los Angeles, appropriates at will from both African American and Latino culture, though it is decidedly African American in its presentation, and thereby serves as the public model of the urban Black male in all his contradictory forms.

Hispanics Causin' Panic

American Me demonstrates that aspects of African American gangsta life and Mexican American gangsta culture are in dialogue with one another, though it can at times be a highly contested dialogue. There are two distinct instances in the film where a potential clash between the races is openly criticized as being counterproductive to someone's coming to consciousness and ultimate cultural empowerment. As the Mexican mafia (La Eme) smuggles drugs into the prison, we witness a Black inmate who steals the cocaine intended for another inmate. Upon revelation of the culprit, Santana, the leader of La Eme, instructs his soldiers to burn the man as an act of punishment. This triggers a cell-block confrontation that borders on a riot between La Eme and the Black Guerrilla Family (BGF). As the prison guards descend, the riot is aborted, but not without critical commentary. Santana informs the leader of the BGF that the situation was not racially motivated, but simply an action of retribution to forestall any future attempts at hindering their drug-trafficking efforts in prison. In other words, "business, never personal." This is a case in which the interest of underground capitalism supersedes any specific racial agenda.

Yet this scene is important as the setup for a similar situation that occurs later in the film. When La Eme attempts to sever its tie with the traditional Italian Mafia, the move is met with much resistance. Scagnelli, the mob boss, refuses to relinquish his end of the drug business in East L.A. As a result, several members of La Eme rape and murder Scagnelli's son while he is in prison. In response, Scagnelli sends uncut heroin into the barrio, causing several overdoses. This creates a chain reaction of retribution, which eventually culminates in Santana's death at the hands of his own men. At a certain point during this series of events, J. D., the only white member of La Eme, who slowly attempts to wrest control of the gang from Santana, orders a hit on the BGF by using the Aryan Brotherhood, the white gang represented in the film. Santana objects to this action and criticizes J. D. for "sending out the wrong message."

Santana's objection is based on his increasing awareness of racial and social consciousness, which has been facilitated by the politically em-powered female character Julie. Julie, like the female character of Ronnie in *Menace*, helps Santana to realize the error of his misguided ways. On several occasions she criticizes his violent philosophy in ways that other characters cannot for fear of death. In a pivotal scene late in the film, Julie exposes Santana's position in all its limitations. After a series of extremely critical remarks about Santana's hypocritical use of crime as a way of arguing for *la raza*, he tells her, "If you were a man, I'd . . . " His incomplete sentence is cut short by Julie's own completion of it: "You'd kill me; no, you'd fuck me in the ass." Having witnessed several scenes in which men were raped because of Santana's power over them, in addition to his rape of Julie, we can feel the magnitude of her statement. She not only criticizes his politics, she has criticized his masculinity by alluding to the latent homosexuality of his supposed gestures of power.

Ultimately, she forces Santana to understand that the power struggles which often take place between those who are marginalized permit the continued oppression of their voices by those in power. Santana even says to J. D., "We spend all our time dealing with the miatas [their slang term for Blacks], and the Aryan Brotherhood, only to be dealing with ourselves." In other words, ideological distractions ultimately leave us in the same place, with no advancement in consciousness or power.

These ideas eventually separate Santana's newfound political consciousness from J. D.'s "business as usual" approach to crime and the underlying destruction of the community. It is not coincidental that J. D.'s whiteness, which is endorsed by Santana early in the film, looms as the final authority once he has ordered the killing of Santana and presumably taken control of the gang. At the beginning of the film, as expressed through the American military oppression of the Mexican American citizens, and at the conclusion, with J. D.'s murdering of Santana, thus destroying any possibility for an overall group consciousness, we can see that racism and white supremacy are the root causes of the chaos that permeates much of the present-day urban landscape. It is this fundamental understanding of race, racism, and complicity in one's own oppression that substantiates the importance of *American Me*. *American Me* engages history and politics to subtly yet convincingly argue that the real root of evil in American society as it relates to oppressed minorities is the bondage of systemic and institutionalized racism. This understanding also distinguishes it as a political statement from the rather limited bourgeois politics of *Boyz n the Hood* and the nihilistically apolitical *Menace II Society*.

This film demonstrates the broad context of gangsta culture, in a sense using the Mexican American discourse to expose the limitations of the two African American films. The two communities are constantly in a cross-cultural dialogue. This exchange is best understood by looking at the culture and iconography of gangsta rap. Latino rappers have continually attempted to use the African American medium of rap to express their own urban male angst. The most obvious examples are East Los Angeles rapper Kid Frost, who raps through the closing credit sequence in *American Me*, and the platinum record–selling Los Angeles–area group Cypress Hill. On the other hand, the Latino car culture, especially "low riding," has been absorbed by the African American gangsta culture, as highlighted in several rap music videos, especially those of Dr. Dre. Interestingly, the strong emphasis on smoking "the chronic" (marijuana), originally celebrated on the albums and in the films of the multiracial comedy team Cheech and Chong in the 1970s, has had a resurgence in gangsta rap initially popularized by Cypress Hill, but carried to extreme proportions with Dr. Dre, Snoop Doggy Dog, Mista Grimm, and the Luniz, all Black rap acts from the West Coast.

In *Menace II Society* we see Caine and O-Dog, after having been physically abused by the police, dropped off in the enemy territory of a Latino barrio, only to be taken to the hospital by the *ese*. This gesture of support, much like Santana's criticism of racism against African Americans, suggests at one level the Hughes brothers' admiration for Olmos's film, but at another level underscores the attempts at dialogue between distinct sets of marginalized voices, as opposed to the perpetration of racial hostility between African Americans and Latinos.

Boyz Will Be Boyz

> Either they don't know, won't show, or don't care
> what's going on in the hood.
>
> —Doughboy, *Boyz n the Hood*

While *American Me* serves as an "objective third party" against which to evaluate *Boyz* and *Menace*, the similarities notwithstanding, to engage the culturally specific tenets of Black popular culture we must look at texts which are firmly situated in the domain of African American cinema in order to study the class politics of each film. In this regard, the political position of *Boyz n the Hood* can be defined as either a bourgeois Black nationalist or an Afrocentric model that focuses on the "disappearing" Black male, yet also fits easily into the perceived pathology of the culture in a modernized version of the legendary Moynihan report of the late 1960s. This report regarded the typically broken African American family as a cause of societal dysfunction at the highest level.

Singleton's film was integral to the politically charged period of resurgent Black nationalism in the late 1980s and early 1990s. This cultural resurgence of Black nationalism, most closely associated with the work of Public Enemy, KRS-One, and Sister Souljah, also set the tone for the discourse that informed *Do the Right Thing*, as well as many of the debates that emerged after the film's release.

From the outset it is obvious that Singleton's film is conversant with the Afrocentric discourse that permeates much of Black intellectual and cultural life. The film opens by establishing South Central Los Angeles as its geographical, cultural, and political center. Yet the landscape of Los Angeles is a historically specific one. The film begins in 1984, as we quickly spot several campaign posters that support the re-election of President Ronald Reagan—the obvious contradiction of this image being seen in a community such as South Central, which is the type of community most victimized by the racial and class politics of Reagan's first term. Another contradiction is signaled as a young Black male, while looking at an abandoned dead body lying in an alley, gives this political image "the finger." This young character is identified as being closely associated with gang culture. He declares that both of his brothers have been shot, and in turn they are heroic in his mind because they have yet to be killed. His marginal status allows him to recognize at some level that this supreme image of white male authority is in stark contrast to his own existence.

As we enter the classroom, we are presented with another contradiction. The camera pans the student drawings that cover the wall. These pictures contain images of people being shot, police brutality, and other acts that emphasize the daily violence that defines many of the lives in this poor Black community. These images are contradicted by the speech being delivered by the white teacher about the historical importance of the first European "settlers" or "pilgrims" on American soil. Her lecture is on the reasons this country celebrates the Thanksgiving holiday, yet by implication it also articulates the exploitation of America and Native Americans and the ensuing colonization, which was a helpful instrument in establishing the societal hierarchy that we inhabit today.

The ideology that is being discussed is being put into practice through the attitudes and policies of Ronald Reagan. Reagan clearly felt the need to return to some form of these earlier examples of oppression in the course of his presidential career, as his repeated attacks on affirmative action, his support of states' rights, and his overall embrace of positions consistent with right-wing conservatism about race clearly indicated. In a sense, the actions of those who are being celebrated by the teacher, the "pilgrims," have contributed to the conditions of the people depicted in the children's drawings. The film sets up a binary opposition between the conservative politics of America and African Americans' rejection of these oppressive policies. This scene is one of the few in the film in which racism and white supremacy are directly critiqued.

As the scene develops, Tre, the film's main character, confronts his elementary school teacher, asserting that humankind originated in Africa and not in Europe. Yet in his presentation, Tre is criticized not only by his teacher, but by other students as well. The same student who gave Reagan "the finger" completely dissociates himself from Tre's Afrocentric assertion, "We're all from Africa." In response, this child declares, "I ain't from Africa, I'm from Crenshaw Mafia," further linking himself to gang culture through his identification with the set known as "Crenshaw

Mafia." The obvious irony of this scene is that gang affiliation is set in direct conflict with one's racial and cultural identity. It is as if being a gangsta supersedes race, as opposed to being a result of racial and class hierarchies in America.

In this same exchange, we can also hear echoes of Tre's father, Furious, and his lessons on life that recur throughout the film. This is once again set in opposition to the words of the aspiring gangsta's older brothers. This exchange leads to a fight between the two children, underscoring the incompatibility of progressive politics and existence in gangsta culture. Yet through the setting of gangsta culture in opposition to nationalist politics, it becomes clear that this bourgeois understanding ignores the fact that gangsters historically are easily transformed into revolutionaries because of their marginal status in society.

Remarks about the plight of the "Black man" dominate much of Furious's commentary in the film. As critic Michael Dyson has alluded, these comments fit well with the male-centered Afrocentric ideals of thinkers such as Jawanza Kanjufu, Haki Madhabuti, and Molefi Asante. Boyz uses gangsta culture as an alluring spectacle, which is underscored by the film's exaggeratedly violent trailer, but this spectacle is used to engage an Afrocentric critique that denounces the routine slaying of Black men, whether by other gang members or by the police. Boyz makes interesting use of many of the icons of gangsta culture while conducting its Black nationalist critique. The film straddles both areas, opening the door to the ensuing onslaught of gangsta imagery.

In this sense, Boyz is much like the imagery connected with one of its co-stars, Ice Cube. As a rapper, Ice Cube has consistently combined signs of gangsta culture with an ideological perspective that emphasizes a perverted Black nationalist agenda, borrowed primarily from the Nation of Islam. Similarly, Boyz combines gangsta icons with Afrocentrism, ultimately privileging the ideological critique over the iconography. This strain of political discourse was popular during the late 1980s and early 1990s, with Boyz providing a cinematic counterpart to rap music. Singleton's film, though visualizing gangsta culture on a mass scale, is really more acceptable as a political text than as a thesis on the complex gangsta mentality. In many ways, Boyz represents the culmination of this politically resurgent period, as the theme of Black nationalism slowly disappeared from most popular forms shortly thereafter.

Though the film is overtly political, it reflects a bourgeois sense of politics. At the conclusion of the film we see a didactic scroll which tells us that Tre and Brandi, the one utopic Black male/female relationship presented in the film, have ventured off to Morehouse and Spelman

College in Atlanta respectively, to pursue their middle-class dreams far away from South Central L.A. Morehouse and Spelman have often been thought of as the Black equivalent of Harvard or Yale, the historical breeding ground for bourgeois Blackness. The fact that the two colleges are located in Atlanta, the current "mecca" of Black America, underscores the film's flimsy political position. *Boyz n the Hood* demonizes the landscape of Los Angeles while uncritically offering middle-class Atlanta as a metaphoric space where future generations of African Americans can exist free of the obstacles that are depicted in this film.

A Straight-Up Menace

This bourgeois political position advocated by *Boyz n the Hood* is fully realized in the Hughes brothers' *Menace II Society*. The films are as different as their respective directors' personal narratives. With media attention having made the personal histories of the African American film directors of this period an integral part of this current movement, the different paths taken by Singleton and Allen and Albert Hughes become an issue in discussing their films. Singleton is one of a long line of successful Hollywood directors who have graduated from the USC School of Cinema-Television. By the time of the release of Singleton's first film, the university film school–educated African American director had become a tradition of the most recent wave of African American cinema. This characteristic could also be used to locate Singleton in the burgeoning new Black aesthetic that Trey Ellis and Greg Tate lauded in the late 1980s, though his film deals with images from gangsta culture. Singleton is thus the product of a group of artists and intellectuals who grew up fully realizing that the seeming promise of 1960s liberalism was ultimately empty of any sustained political empowerment, though individual access to power was to some extent freed up by the process that would eventually allow a few people some small share of cultural capital, but continue to oppress the Black masses. This sense of entitlement marked by strong disillusion revealed that access to power is still the domain of elite white males.

Boyz n the Hood shares these sentiments. Tre, by virtue of his father's wisdom and guidance, is offered the possibility to achieve some financial success which is presented as a momentary though ultimately unattainable possibility for Ricky and a non-issue altogether for Doughboy. Yet Tre's access to this perceived position of power is clearly marked by a cynical disillusionment that hinders him as a consequence of not only direct racial oppression, but also, and maybe more importantly, an oppression which is rendered that much more difficult by oppression from his own people. This is especially true in light of the recurrent image of the self-hating Black police officer who has been ideologically seduced to believe that his own personal interests are synonymous with those of the white establishment that ultimately oppresses him on the same basis of race. One could argue that the film fails to deal with the historical situation of racist hostility between the violent white officers of the LAPD and its Black victims, which was exposed in the 1991 Rodney King beating. What we see in the film is consistent with Ice Cube's warning in "Fuck tha Police": "Don't let it be a black and a white one / Cause he'll slam you down to the street top / Black police showing out for the white cop." This scenario is clearly visualized for us in the film.

The Hughes brothers, on the other hand, function much more in line with the truly disadvantaged, having had very little formal college education, with only brief community college and technical school experience. Their initial marginality creates a different agenda from the one pursued by Singleton. The Hughes brothers were afforded the opportunity to hone their skills in the assembly line-like process of making rap music videos. Music videos have increasingly become an alternative to the conservative film industry for aspiring creators of African American culture. It is this initial marginality that informs *Menace.*

Thus we have filmmakers from two distinct segments of the African American cultural community. Singleton clearly fits in with the educated elite of the new Black aesthetic who attempt to deal with being consciously Black and middle-class simultaneously and the difficulties of inhabiting what are often complicated and conflicting positions. This dilemma has been played out in differing ways in several arenas of contemporary culture, from the cultural critiques of both *School Daze* and *Jungle Fever*, to the Black nationalism of Chuck D from Public Enemy, to the recent publication of several memoirs by African Americans, including Stephen Carter's *Reflections of an Affirmative Action Baby*, Jill Nelson's *Volunteer Slavery*, Lisa Jones's *Bulletproof Diva*, Jake Lamar's *Bourgeois Blues*, Ellis Cose's *The Rage of a Privileged Class*, Nathan McCall's *Make Me Wanna Holler*, and Shelby Steele's *The Content of Our Character*. While these artists or writers may take different positions on the political issues that are presented, it is Black middle-class angst that informs each of their texts.

The Hughes brothers occupy another strand of contemporary African American cultural production. With several specific references, such as the ominous figure of Ice Cube, we can see the Hughes brothers as part of a lower-class, though activist, tradition that uses their marginality, to invoke bell hooks, as a "site of resistance." The evolution of the gangster to consciousness that we witnessed in the writings of Iceberg Slim in the 1970s has here been revived by the Hughes brothers.

In the cases of both Singleton and the Hughes brothers, varying definitions of Blackness are distinguished by their position on the issue of class. This multiple configuration of race and class marks distinct schools of thought on questions of representation and the production of meaning relative to understanding the function of a broadened context of cultural production. Whereas the issue of representing Blackness may unify these texts for discussion, a class-based analysis can differentiate what can be considered an Afrocentric text from one that foregrounds the gangsta's ethos of nihilistic realism. The spectrum of representational positions relative to contemporary Black culture is alluded to in the title of Nelson George's 1993 book *Buppies, B-Boys, BAPS, and Bohos.* The range of identity from Black urban professionals and Black American princesses to hip-hop B-boys and cultural bohemians only highlights the endless possibilities of African American identity formation in the 1990s.

This film refuses to advocate solutions or make apologies for the difficult situation of contemporary Black male existence; instead, there is a premise of "authenticity" which uses culture to cut off political engagement and in turn present the imagery of gangsta culture in all its "perverted glory." The lower-class ethos of gritty urban realism depicted by the Hughes brothers is offered as the answer to the otherwise (bland by comparison) bourgeois aspirations of Singleton's political film.

In this sense, *Menace* is more in line with the thematics of gangsta culture, which celebrate excess and frown on politics. Throughout the film there are repeated critiques of both religion and presumed Black nationalism. Early on, the main character, Caine, describes the limited vision of Sharif, a character who embraces the rhetoric of the Nation of Islam, though he only hangs out with the gangstas in the film. Caine mockingly derides Sharif for thinking that "Allah could save Black people." In response to a remark made by Caine's overly religious grandfather, Caine's partner, O Dog, laughingly questions that if there is truly a concerned God, why are they living in such "fucked-up" conditions? In addition, the film's lone Black athlete, Stacy, says to the religiously dogmatic Sharif, in response to his suggestion that they play a Muslim lecture on the car stereo, "You better go somewhere with that Black Power shit. You know that shit gets no play in this ride."

These examples are a contemporary version of a memorable scene from *Superfly.* When Priest is confronted by several Black nationalists about his need to "pay some dues" to the community, he responds by chastising them on the ineffectiveness of their struggle: "When you get some guns, I'll be the first one down on the front line, killing whitey. But until then, you can go sing your marching songs somewhere else." These overt rejections of religious and political discourse demonstrate that gangsta culture functions as the complete opposite of more ideologically minded projects.

Another aspect of *Menace* that directly responds to *Boyz* has to do with the denial of a privileging parental voice, as these familial figures are quickly erased from the film's narrative. Caine, the film's main character, is both a motherless and a fatherless child; his parents were the victims of a drug overdose and a murder, respectively. His grandparents, who have raised him, can offer nothing but the status quo position on the troubled life of a young black male such as Caine. In one scene, Caine stares off aimlessly as his grandfather scolds him, while we see from a low-angle camera position the contradictory image of a "blue-eyed Jesus" on the wall above. Caine's disinterest is further underscored by *It's a Wonderful Life*, which plays on the television. His grandparents' inability to move beyond their own place in mainstream America leaves him with no generational voice of wisdom such as Tre's character has in *Boyz*. Caine is left to his own devices, which ultimately lead to his death.

Whereas *Boyz* clearly suggests that those who follow the advice of their fathers have an advantage over those who have no father at all, *Menace* is equally emphatic in suggesting that all things come to a bitter end, regardless. The only consistent politically empowered male voice in the film, Mr. Butler, offers words of wisdom to both Caine and his own son Sharif, yet both end up as victims in the film's tragic ending. Equally interesting is that the voice of Black rage in the film, O Dog, flees the final shootout and remains alive, while his friends, all ambivalent about the gangsta lifestyle, end up dead.

Menace, in union with the overall ideology of Dr. Dre, refuses to give an ideological explanation for the violent culture that it represents. Instead, it uses cinematic spectacle to depict this culture in all its blighted glory. Repeated references to Hollywood provide larger-than-life images that define the very existence of the characters. During one of the early house party scenes, we witness an exchange between Caine's father and one of the guests, who has just returned home from prison. Caine's father angrily asks for money which he is owed, suggesting that the character has been out of prison long enough to have paid his debt. In response, the man sarcastically asks, "Who the fuck do you think you are, nigga, Ron O'Neal or something?" The actor who became famous for his starring role in *Superfly*, Ron O'Neal, in a direct reference to 1970s African American popular culture, is invoked as an example of supreme defiance and ultramasculinity.

This fascination with Hollywood imagery is furthered through the use of the most apparent symbol of this infatuation with spectacle, the security camera videotape. At the beginning of the film we witness an enraged O Dog kill the owners of a Korean liquor store and then confiscate the tape that has recorded the murders. Instead of suppressing the tape, O Dog begins showing it to all of his homeys as a way of displaying his prowess as a killer. While Caine is concerned that the tape will lead to their arrest, O Dog is defiant in using it to place himself in the company of the world's most notorious killers. As several of the homeys congratulate O Dog on his newfound celebrity, he declares, "I'm larger than that nigga Steven Segal," clearly demonstrating that his actions have escalated him above the fictional beacon of Hollywood masculinity, Segal.

As the film nears its conclusion, Caine is offered the opportunity to move to Atlanta with his new girlfriend, Ronnie. In response to her suggestion, and, by extension, in an obvious response to Singleton, Caine replies by denouncing the utopic aspirations implied through Atlanta: "You act like Atlanta ain't in America. They don't give a fuck." This political critique of American racism, and the suggestion that the problems of contemporary existence are much too complex to simply walk away from, stands out in a film which endeavors not to be political.

Unlike *Boyz*, which finds strength in its script, *Menace* uses all of the tools of the cinema to visually choreograph what turns out to be a death march. While it is difficult to remember anything arrestingly visual about the Singleton film, the Hughes brothers use the cinematic medium to produce pure spectacle that ultimately conceals any thematic limitations the film might otherwise be accused of having. For instance, a routine police chase of African American youth is turned into the type of deliberate pursuit often associated with Olympic track footage or seen in the film *Chariots of Fire*. The processing of crack cocaine for profit is shown in minute cinematic detail to the accompaniment of NWA's "Dope Man." A 1970s ghetto party is depicted in blue light, capturing the true essence of soul along with the echoes of "Iceman" Jerry Butler proclaiming that "only the strong survive," a prophetic reminder for the film and for all those who are asleep to the ways of life in the 'hood.

Menace II Society is truly a "beautiful" film, yet one wonders how something this tragic can at the same time be described as beautiful. The Hughes brothers have managed to expose the perversity of urban lower-class black male existence while refusing to critique it. Thus, the film functions as pure celebration devoid of the political baggage of

Boyz. As a way of underscoring this celebration, the film opens with documentary footage of the 1965 Watts riots, yet no connection is drawn between those historical occurrences and the instances that dominate the rest of the text. It is as if the footage is there simply to remind us that the event happened—a use of historical spectacle for the sake of spectacle.

Olmos makes similar use of a "riot" in *American Me*. The 1942 "Zoot Suit" riots begin Olmos's investigation into the depths of Mexican American life in East Los Angeles. Yet in *American Me*, the riots are specifically connected to the personal lives of the characters. Instead of using historical footage, Olmos opts for a fictional re-creation of the events that places the main character, Santana, in the midst of racial discourse in postwar Los Angeles. Part of the film's brilliance lies in its ability to fuse personal history with public history, to link the issues of private discourse with a discourse that encompasses the society as a whole. It is this linking of public and private, the historical and the everyday, that distinguishes *American Me* from both *Boyz n the Hood* and *Menace II Society.*

Boyz n the Hood has its filmic heart in the right place, though the actions of the film dictate something entirely different. Singleton's debut is indeed worthy of much praise, especially considering its massive box-office appeal and its ability to bring together the lingering fragments of its era in a cohesive whole. The film is very much a modern-day *Superfly* in that it will continue to represent the major social and political concerns of its time for many years to come. Yet we cannot ignore the film's political limitations in the interest of praising a positive and much-needed African American effort.

Menace II Society, on the other hand, celebrates the excesses of gangsta culture in such an illuminating fashion that we tend to forget the real horrors of this lifestyle. Quentin Tarantino has been similarly successful in turning grotesque violence into comedic spectacle, as has Hong Kong filmmaker John Woo by using the cinema and the portrayal of violence as choreographed performance art. In each case, the violence is less about physical destruction and more a convenient vehicle for the expression of spectacle in a hyperreal sense. In addition, the nihilism associated with this film, and ultimately this lifestyle, can be read somewhat politically even though it works to discourage the traditional discourse of politics.

Menace is such a powerful film that I often am caught between criticizing its rather obvious shortcomings and being sutured by the stunning visuals. The real violence of everyday life in post industrial Los Angeles is often lost in the process. The nihilism that informs the film is problematic on one level, as numerous African American gatekeepers will surely attest, but I take those popular critiques to be dismissive and not fully elaborative. Yet as Paul Gilroy has stated in his reading of contemporary African American life, "nihilism ceases to be antisocial and becomes social in the obvious sense of the term: it generates community and specifies the fortified boundaries of racial particularity" (68).

I focus on the cinematic dimension in conjunction with the gangsta ethos as articulated through rap music so as to define the film as an "authentic" voice of the truly disadvantaged, and maybe because this has historically been a voice absent from Hollywood cinema, I see it as providing a much-needed service. Again the problem stems from a lack of other forms of representation and the monolithic nature accorded African American culture. This is not intended as a defense as much as it is a position statement on the perverted state of contemporary culture. In this case I agree with Tricia Rose, who says, "The forces that constrain black agency must be acknowledged while the spirit and reality of black free will must be preserved" (142).

It is important to look at these films as part of a larger cultural matrix that links issues of race and class so as to fully understand the complex nature of gangsta culture and its representation in mainstream society. If we look to the three films as enhancing each other's strengths and critiquing each other's limitations, we can start to envision an empowered articulation of marginality that defies the monolithic reduction of race often rendered by dominant media discourse.

To suggest that the political but bourgeois leanings of *Boyz n the Hood* are enhanced by the cinematically apolitical "pure" spectacle of *Menace II Society*, and that both have a solid ideological foundation that exposes the historical effects of white supremacy on racialized others through *American Me*, is to appreciate the cross-cultural specificity of postmodern Los Angeles and the important contribution of cinema to this dialogue.

True to the Game:
Basketball as the Embodiment of Blackness
in Contemporary Popular Culture

White men can't jump? They don't have to. They own the team.

—Paul Mooney, Comedian

The game of basketball has come to be an integral part of American and African American culture. Television commercials feature basketball players, basketball players were regular guests on the formerly popular *Arsenio Hall Show* and to this day are often seen on both *The Tonight Show with Jay Leno* and *The Late Show with David Letterman*, and certain celebrity ballplayers such as Michael Jordan, Magic Johnson, Charles Barkley, and Shaquille O'Neal have evolved beyond the world of their sport to become popular American icons. Further, the moving documentary *Hoop Dreams* (1994), about the plight of two Chicago youth attempting to make a career out of their dream to become basketball superstars, documents the intense competition in the game and the important place that it occupies for so many people in this society.

However, basketball has much to say about contemporary African American culture, especially as a way of understanding race, class, and masculinity. This chapter will explore the sport as a site of struggle relative to the racial and class dilemmas that define much contemporary discourse in this country. My analysis will look at the game in its present form as an extension of Black popular culture, similar to jazz in an earlier era, though the game has seldom been treated critically in the study of cultural forms. Finally, I will look at the class politics that define the game, in a sport where race has been normalized through performance, and class, specifically the class politics of the nigga, starts to assume a prominent position in articulating Black masculinity. Ultimately I will argue that basketball, like gangsta rap and gangsta cinema, is a primary venue for the representation of a truly disadvantaged Black male aesthetic, one that many scholars of popular culture tend to ignore.

Basketball as a Contemporary Site of Struggle

One of the pivotal scenes in Spike Lee's *Do the Right Thing* (1989) foregrounds the game of basketball as a site of struggle relative to the question of race and identity politics in contemporary American society. In an often-repeated scene, we witness the volatile character Buggin' Out as his new Air Jordan basketball shoes are inadvertently stepped on by one of the few white residents in the neighborhood. This scene is instructive with respect to the racial hierarchy that exists in the game of basketball and in American society as a whole.

Buggin' Out wears an important symbol of Blackness in contemporary commodity culture, Air Jordans, the shoes that encapsulate the mediated image of basketball superstar and American icon Michael Jordan. Michael Dyson describes Jordan through the "spectacle-laden black athletic body as the site of commodified black cultural imagination" (*Reflecting Black*, 70). Jordan's prowess both as a basketball player and as an icon of popular commodity culture is most visibly expressed through the ubiquitous shoes, which have become popular as the result of a series of celebrated television commercials over the last ten years. By owning a pair of Air Jordans, Buggin' Out, like a large segment of American and African American youth culture, owns a metaphoric piece of Michael Jordan, thus demonstrating the cultural currency with which Blackness is exchanged.

What makes this scene interesting, though, is that the white character, played by John Savage, is wearing a Boston Celtics jersey bearing the name and number of Larry Bird. Bird, in contrast to Jordan, was visible in spite of doing few commercials. His visibility had to do with his whiteness. As a white male, he worked in a game which is one of the few cultural arenas in this society dominated by Black male participants.[1]

The verbal confrontation that ensues subtly references the battle for dominance and power, specific to the question of race, in the National Basketball Association (NBA). The central issue in this scene revolves around the occupation and violation of space, both personal and public. Savage's character, on the one hand, is defined not only by his Celtic jersey, but equally by his ownership of a brownstone in this all-Black neighborhood. The fact that this image is closely tied into the image of Larry Bird specifically, and whiteness in general, articulates the cultural politics that is here implied.

Bird, as represented by the John Savage character, is the most recent example of the "great white hope," a phrase used in the early part of the century to describe the numerous white competitors to the heavy-weight boxing throne of champion Jack Johnson. As the flamboyant Johnson's prowess in the ring increased, several boxing promoters and many members of the white public sought a "white hope" with the ability to defeat him, feeling that a Black champion was socially unac-ceptable. Following Johnson's reign, the sport of boxing often attempted to resurrect this iconic figure, notably in the form of Rocky Marciano, Gerry Cooney, and most recently Tommy Morrison. This situation is effectively dramatized in the Martin Ritt film *The Great White Hope* (1972).

A number of white athletes have since been given this label as they have attempted to unseat various African American superstars in the world of sports. Larry Bird is one of the most recent embodiments of this tradition. This difference with Bird is that he was very good at the game, while many of the other white competitors could be summarized as truly no more than a "hope."

Bird's success in the NBA notwithstanding, his larger-than-life status reflected the latent politics of race that defined the league during his tenure. As a player, Bird was often described as limited in his physical gifts, such as running and jumping, but this description was more than compensated for when his overall *game* was referred to. Commentators discussed his exceptional work ethic, his amazing grasp of the game's fundamentals, his immense knowledge of the game, and his overall intelligence. Larry Bird was possibly the only player in the league who could turn a simple pass into an intellectual endeavor of the highest order. Bird's representation fits in neatly with the stereotypes often linked with white athletes, those of intelligence, hard work, and perseverance, traits which are often celebrated as fundamental to good citizenship in American society.

Michael Jordan's presence in this scene is implied through the Air Jordan basketball shoes. Buggin' Out is defined by his shoes, the expensive commodity which is indelibly linked with the image of Michael Jordan. The difference here between owning shoes and owning property reflects the established racial hierarchy both in the film and in society as a whole. Though Jordan may be a highly popular image and make great sums of money, his status and access to the corridors of power, though obviously higher than those of most African Americans, are still subordinate to the corporate interests that he represents commercially.

In the same way, Jordan is somewhat subordinate to Bird, whose whiteness links him with the owners of the various franchises, who ultimately control the game. Buggin' Out claims that John Savage has no business in his neighborhood, yet Savage actually owns property, while Buggin' Out assumes that the neighborhood belongs to him simply by virtue of his occupation of it. Much like the Bloods and Crips, who lay claim to significant areas of South Central Los Angeles that they may occupy by force and intimidation yet to which they have no real rights of ownership, the disturbing reality of this situation is that Black people's ownership is often limited to trivial items that have no real value outside of demonstrating their slave-like relationship to commodity culture. This also relates directly to the NBA, as Black players have defined the league from an aesthetic and performance standpoint, but remain excluded from full access to power in the form of ownership.[2]

Jordan occupied a different position from Bird's in the pantheon of the NBA. Jordan was often celebrated for his gravity-defying leaps and his highly stylized moves to the basket. This emphasis on the physical is highlighted in three CBS/Fox home videos devoted to his exploits, *Come Fly with Me*, *Michael Jordan's Playground*, and most recently *Air Time*. These videos demonstrate Jordan's embodiment of the popular phrase "human highlight film."

An obvious difference between Bird and Jordan is that the white performer is defined by traditional American ideology. The image of Horatio Alger is invoked, much like the discourse surrounding that quintessential white sports icon Rocky, which describes an athlete from working-class origins who pulls himself up by his bootstraps through sacrifice and hard work at the expense of a Black champion who clearly needs to be "put in his place." Bird's presumed intelligence clearly affirms his upward social trajectory. This image is ironic because in the real life of sports advertising, Bird's lower-class demeanor was considered a liability, and he therefore was unable to attract many endorsements early in his career, the result of an obvious inability to clearly articulate his speech.

The real-life circumstances of Larry Bird the individual seem to inform these glowing descriptions of his playing style. Bird was born and raised in the rural, working-class confines of French Lick, Indiana. He initially attended Indiana University, but according to legend he was thrown off the team by celebrated college coach Bob Knight, after which he became a sanitation worker until he enrolled at the lesser-known school Indiana State University. Bird had an outstanding career at Indiana State, a small school with an unheard-of basketball team, taking them to the NCAA finals his senior year. This championship game pitted Bird's team against Michigan State Spartans and the man who would become his professional nemesis, Magic Johnson. After losing to Michigan State, Bird went on to become a famed player for Boston.

In the NBA, which is dominated by African American players, Bird provided a departure. He was a self-described "white man in a Black man's game," truly a rarity when we consider the minimal number of "games" we could describe as belonging to Black men in American society. Yet racial politics are fundamental to understanding the importance of basketball as an extension of African American culture.

The Social Construction of Winning

The racial politics between Bird and Jordan, and by extension the racial politics that define the game itself, are interestingly summarized in a line from Ron Shelton's *White Men Can't Jump* (1992). Woody Harrelson's character, Billy Hoyle, the "white man" in question, states to Wesley Snipes's character, Sidney Dean, that Black and white players differ because "white men would rather look bad and win, while Black men would rather look good and lose."

There are several implied assumptions in this statement. Overtly it assumes that Black men, and thus Black culture, are more interested in form as opposed to a white interest in content. Concurrently there is an assumed Black obsession with style, while white culture seems to be inclined more toward substance. These assumptions are not too far from the old racist statement that white people are superior intellectually, while Blacks possess superior physical abilities. Thus the statement in the film is indeed problematic. Yet there is another possible reading which suggests that because the concept of "winning" is an elusive one, as white men control the ability to redefine it for their own purposes at will, Black men have instead opted for something they can control, which in this case happens to be style.

The Detroit Pistons teams of the late 1980s and early 1990s became highly successful by playing in a style that had clearly evolved from the depths of Black culture. The game of basketball stands out for its emphasis on offense, yet the Pistons emphasized defense in their climb into the league's elite. With a style similar to that of gangsta rap, the Pistons brought a menacing and aggressive, hard-nosed, no-bend, defense that many criticized for being too violent. The team (and its style) became known as the "Bad Boys," using the image of physical intimidation to dominate the league.

While there was an overwhelming majority of Black players on this team in this Blackest of American cities, thus allowing for the easy facilitation of the racial subtext of violence, the two most visible white contributors to the team, coach Chuck Daly and player Bill Laimbeer, were equally associated with Blackness in one way or another. Daly had a propensity for wearing fashions thought of as being "Black" in style and emblematic of a gangster; thus the players' nickname for him was "Daddy Rich." The only white player of any stature on the team, Laimbeer was widely thought of as "the most hated man in the league" for his extremely aggressive style of play, which often resulted in fights with other players.

By relying on this aggressive style of defense, the Pistons substantially reduced the scores of the games, making the networks nervous, as high-scoring games and marquee offensive players help sell the league to viewing consumers. While the Pistons were winning in the traditional sense, they were losing by not conforming to the standards set by those in power. Thus, when their reign ended to Michael Jordan's Bulls in 1991, many associated with the league breathed a sigh of relief. In an extensive *Playboy* interview from 1992, Jordan himself says: "The Pistons will knock you down, then, if possible, kick you. They try to use that crap as an intimidator. The evil came out of their attitude, the unsportsmanlike actions. That bad-boy image brought them some gold, but it also brought them a lot of shame" (Diehl, 56). In addition, when the Olympic "Dream Team" was picked in 1992, Piston star Isiah Thomas was visibly excluded. Many concluded that Thomas's omission was revenge for his role as leader of the "Bad Boys," and the tarnish that this group brought to the league and its attempt to maintain a clean image.

In light of the images of violence, decline, and decay associated with the urban landscape in a city such as Detroit, it is not surprising that the image associated with the team emphasized Blackness in a negative sense. Thus as the Pistons dominated the league for several years, their winning ways were actually downplayed in comparison to some of the other teams who were winning during the same period. Detroit, defined by an empowered sense of Blackness, both in its essence and in the team's style of play, was judged by a different set of standards from those normally associated with winning. And as Billy adds in *White Men*, "Sometimes when you win you really lose, and sometimes when you lose you really win."

From Bebop to B-Ball:
Basketball as a Contemporary Version of Jazz

Basketball players often talk about their "game," by which they mean their overall approach to playing basketball, both physical and mental. Much like musicians who talk about their "music" or filmmakers discussing their "films," basketball players regard their abilities in much the same way, as a craft. This definition of physical activity as art is a radical departure from the elitist definitions often associated with the concept of art in Western culture.

Basketball has come to serve many of the same functions in contemporary society that jazz did in an earlier period. The articulation of jazz from the mid-1940s to the late 1960s marked an important period in the history of both American and African American culture. From the advent of bebop through the last days of acoustic-based jazz, there was a community of musicians who defined their own culture based upon ideas that came forth from the oral idiom that they practiced.

A good example can be found in innovative jazz pianist Thelonious Monk. Any attempt at reducing Monk's music to mere notes would be not only impossible, but disrespectful to the vastness of his work. Monk, as the Charlotte Zwerin film *Straight, No Chaser* (1989) reveals, is a complex artist whose transcendence of the seemingly small world of music is a testament to the impact of his distinguished body of work. Monk's contribution to the canon of African American art and culture, as well as his significance in terms of American art and culture in the twentieth century, is something that will be intellectually pursued for years to come.

Basketball superstar Michael Jordan embodies what I have often called *the fusion of the formal and the vernacular* in the same way that jazz did years earlier.[3] His ability to play the best of "textbook" basketball, along with his ability to nuance this formal performance through his reliance on the tenets of Black oral culture as they relate to the game, sets him apart as an innovator and a cultural icon of unmatched status.[4]

Jordan clearly transcends the world of basketball, as Monk did the world of music, having entered into a rare cultural domain, especially when you consider that he is a Black man in a society that has often attempted to erase African American males from the landscape. Though it is difficult to reduce Jordan's career or iconic status to a singular episode, one feat of improvisation on his part substantiates my argument that basketball is the modern-day aesthetic embodiment of Black culture, similar to jazz in its prime.

In game three of the 1991 NBA finals pitting Chicago against the Los Angeles Lakers, Jordan executed a miraculous move, gliding through the lane and switching shooting hands from his right to his left while in midair, and finally laying the ball up successfully, much to the amazement of the other players and the adoring audience, both those in the arena and those watching on television. Author Sam Smith of *The Jordan Rules* described this shot as "art, poetry without words, an instant for eternity" (333). Jordan, who was trying to evade the notoriously long arms of his opponent Sam Perkins, had visually exemplified an impulse normally defined from an oral perspective. His ability to switch gears— or, in the parlance of gangsta rap, "flip the script"—on the spot, is a firm indication that the game of basketball when played in this way is truly about improvisation and the resulting Black cultural ethos that goes along with it.

As Jordan has often suggested, it was necessary for him to "raise his game to a higher level." This notion of a higher level is reminiscent of Mahalia Jackson's evocative rendition of the gospel tune "Move On Up a Little Higher." Jackson bought the genre of gospel into the modern era, proof of her ability to fuse jazz-like arrangements with the aesthetic domain specific to gospel music. Though "Move On Up a Little Higher" is very much a gospel tune thematically, its implications for African American culture are multiple.

The concept of elevating culture is at the root of what gets transferred across time, be it Monk, Miles Davis, Duke Ellington, or John Coltrane. In this case, though, Jordan's ability to "take his game to a higher level" can be read as an attempt to elevate the artistry of African American culture in both social and political terms: a sophisticated advancement on a preexisting form of discourse.

Toward a Black Aesthetic of Basketball

As jazz was becoming less and less relevant in the 1970s as the result of a number of factors, especially the decline of music education in the public school systems across America, basketball, like hip-hop, was experiencing a rise in importance to the articulation of a distinctly Black aesthetic.

As is usually the case with African American culture, its defiance of the core of Western society deems that those things which might be considered problematic in one context enter an entirely different domain when specified according to race. As a consequence of the limited opportunities for African Americans to participate in the "legitimate" art world in the past, we have often seen a renegotiation of those arenas that were available. This is best represented in music, as African Americans have clearly made significant contributions to or been a major influence on every genre of music to emerge in twentieth-century America. Yet seldom have we in the critical world considered the importance of sports, especially basketball, as a means of demonstrating cultural aesthetics.

Much of the critical dialogue about African American culture in the late 1960s and early 1970s revolved around identifying a distinctly "Black aesthetic." These concerns are most effectively presented in the Addison Gayle anthology *The Black Aesthetic* (1971). Much as Alain Locke's *The New Negro* served as a manifesto for the Harlem Renaissance in the 1920s, Gayle's text would occupy a similar position for the Black arts and aesthetic movement. Several African American artists and intellectuals engaged in dialogue about the importance of specifying those things that defined Black culture. While the intellectual exchange behind these debates should be lauded, history has revealed many of these concerns to be limited by a strong sense of essentialism. Contemporary society has taught us that there is no exclusive way of defining "Blackness," though I would argue that certain criteria must be in place. The heart of these criteria is the sustained articulation of an oral culture, which is most often presented in the form of improvisation. Thus, jazz is an obvious signifier of African American culture.

This oral culture has always made style a distinct component of its presentation, as Hoyt Fuller alludes in his opening chapter from the Gayle text, "Towards a Black Aesthetic." According to Fuller's definition, sports exemplifies these desired aesthetic qualities. Fuller singles out Jim Brown's "lazy amble" back to the huddle, Big Daddy Lipscomb's "making sideline tackles in full view of the crowd and the way, after crushing a ball carrier to the ground, he would chivalrously assist him to his feet," as well as what he describes as "the constant cool of Satchel Paige" (10). He goes on to mention Muhammad Ali, Sugar Ray Robinson, and Archie Moore as other examples who exhibit a certain style in the pursuit of their athletic endeavors.

While Fuller's list is specific to the historical period in which he writes, he fails to mention any basketball players. Undoubtedly there were players such as Bill Russell, Oscar Robinson, and Wilt Chamberlain who could easily have been noted, but Fuller's oversight probably had to do with the relative immaturity of basketball as a venue for the expression of a Black aesthetic and, maybe more important, the absence of any notion that basketball could even fit into the Black aesthetic dimension.

What is interesting, though, is that as Fuller's work was being published, basketball was on its way to becoming an exclusively African American domain of creativity. While the 1960s saw an increase in the number of African American males getting scholarships to play ball at elite colleges previously resistant to integration, the 1970s would see the proliferation of these players in the professional ranks. This increased representation, much like the increase in the number of Black males in the game of baseball after Jackie Robinson's "breaking of the color line" in 1947, gradually brought a change in the way the game was to be played.

As the 1970s progressed, African American participation in basketball increased in two ways. First, the National Basketball Association, the oldest and most established professional league, absorbed many of the players coming out of the noted college programs. The NBA played a more formalized game consistent with the league's traditional style that had been established through the years.

The other, increasingly prominent professional league during this time was the fledgling American Basketball Association (ABA). According to Nelson George in *Elevating the Game*, the ABA, described as "dominated by a Black athletic aesthetic" (181), began in 1967, and through its relatively short-lived existence (1967–1976) made two important contributions to the game of basketball with respect to advancing the style of play.

First of all, the existence of the ABA gave more players, especially Black players, an opportunity to play the game. Secondly, because of this increase in Black player personnel and the less restrictive form of play, the style of the game was subtly nuanced into a more open-court, fast-paced version. These two factors would later affect the NBA, as four of the ABA teams, and many of its best players, merged with the NBA in 1977.

As a direct result of access to major universities gained through the civil rights movement in the 1960s, larger numbers of African American males were given college scholarships to play basketball. This increase in the potential labor pool for the professional leagues provided the ABA with the bodies needed to propel the league forward. Obviously, with more job opportunities, more African Americans were given a chance to make large sums of money playing a game, as opposed to filling slots in an always racially contested job market outside the sports and entertainment fields. This situation, along with a similar one in football, created a popular rags-to-riches sports mythology, especially as a venue for African American participation, as *Hoop Dreams* (1994) depicts impressively. Yet it also aided in the evolution of basketball as the sport of choice for many African American participants and spectators. Like jazz before it, basketball now had a substantial body of cultural producers who, through their communal exchange, spurred by competition, created a distinct style and aesthetic specific to African American culture.

This increase in Black participation came at a time when the ABA was seeking to distinguish itself from the more traditional NBA. The difference came in the form of a more open style of play, which concentrated on a "transition" game that rapidly moved up and down the court, as well as the novelty of three-point shots and the centrality of the dunk, making for a faster-paced game that relied on athletic skills such as running and jumping. In this sense, the game became akin to an improvisational jazz performance, where players were forced to produce spontaneously, instead of the more classically oriented NBA game, which relied more on running set plays.

Since that time, some would even suggest that African American participation in the game has produced a conflict between "textbook" basketball and "playground" basketball. The term "textbook" implies a structured formality in which adherence to a specific set of rules determines one's ability to play successfully and "correctly." Thus heavy reliance on a series of repeated plays dictates the best players and best teams. The Boston Celtics, the most traditional of all the NBA franchises, have always been strong proponents of the textbook style of play.[5] In the same way, Boston as a city has often been viewed as traditional and conservative. The Boston Red Sox, the city's baseball franchise, were the last major-league team to include African American players on their roster. In addition, the racial hysteria surrounding school busing in the 1970s and the more recent case of Charles Stuart, who murdered his wife for insurance money and blamed an anonymous "Black man," lend credence to the city's extremely conservative image. Thus the extension of this conservative racial imagery to the game of basketball appears to be a logical one.

In contrast to this rather restrictive style of play is the much more open style often referred to as "playground." With direct reference to an urban environment, playground signifies the racial coding of this term. While "textbook" implies a classroom or some sort of academic environment, and by extension the connotation of whiteness, the playground can be seen to represent the inner city, and thus is associated almost exclusively with African Americans. Because of the informal nature of pick-up basketball played on the playground—no referees, time clock, etc.—the game becomes determined almost purely by those things created in the course of the game. Though a cursory knowledge of the rules of basketball is important, the actual rules are determined on a case-by-case basis. In other words, the rules are not there to hinder the game, but instead they serve as a subtle form of enforcement when necessary. What is paramount is the creativity inherent in this liberal style of performance.

A primary exemplar of "playground" basketball would be the Los Angeles Laker teams from the 1979–80 season through the 1990–91 season, or roughly during the initial Magic Johnson era. Johnson's renowned ability to run the fast break centers on his talent for improvising with the basketball, creating on the run and alternating plays with split-second accuracy. This highly stylized form of play was underscored by the Lakers' nickname during this period, "Showtime." Simultaneously referencing the Hollywood-like aura that surrounded the team, its location in the city of spectacle, Los Angeles, and the team's spectacular playing style, "Showtime" reinforces the split between textbook and playground, especially in light of the fact that the Lakers' primary competition during this time was the more traditional Boston Celtics.

Textbook basketball is akin to classical music, wherein performance is centered on the replication of a supposedly superior style. Musical sophistication is determined by one's proximity to the original; deviations are considered errors. This privileging of the original seems to permeate much of Western culture. Mastery of the form is achieved through one's ability to replicate at the highest level. With this in mind, those who operate in the tradition of textbook basketball can be clearly linked to this recurrent Western ethos of replication.

Playground basketball, on the other hand, is much like jazz in the sense that mastery of form depends upon one's ability to improvise, to create on the spot, to engage in full-court transition games that foreground style. The celebration of style through improvisation, consistent with much of African American culture, has had a great impact on the selling of the NBA to the American public through the mass media in the 1980s and into the 1990s.

A Whole New Ball Game

As the NBA moved into the 1990s, a new breed of player began to dominate its ranks. Though Michael Jordan was still the league's central producer and commercial selling point, the eventual retirement of Larry

Bird and the forced (albeit temporary) retirement of Magic Johnson, who had contracted HIV, opened the way for new players who would attempt to take the league to the next level. This new generation of players would inherit the benefits of playing what had become America's premier sport in terms of media popularity, corporate sponsorship, and overall visibility.

This unprecedented level of popularity was clearly due to the presence of the highly visible Jordan, but also, over time, had to do with the declining significance of baseball, which culminated in the abortion of the 1994 season because of the owners' and players' refusal to reach a collective bargaining agreement. Football was still the most popular spectator sport statistically, yet its overall influence also seemed to decline as basketball's style of play evolved and the league continued to modernize its performance to appeal to the visually sophisticated American appetite.

In other words, basketball was a game perfectly suited to the fast-paced visual culture that television now offered on a regular basis, a visual style which had a lot to do with the spectacle of music videos. Basketball, which at its best offers a continuous flow of activity and few interruptions in play, provides a visual display that is punctuated by spectacular dunks and three-point shots. On the evening sports programs such as ESPN's *Sportscenter* and CNN's *Sports Tonight*, which feature highlights from virtually all of the day's sporting events, basketball's spectacular nature works perfectly when distilled to the most visually alluring plays. A few prominent plays can be selected and used as a representation of an entire game, as almost every contest offers several dunks or three-point shots to choose from. Thus an otherwise boring game can be represented as exciting simply through the selection of sensational plays, making the entire game appear to be one continuous spectacle. In today's highly mediated environment, this quality is important.

As football attempts to accommodate this media demand for spectacle and as baseball continually refuses, basketball continues to increase in importance as a form of entertainment. Basketball players are often seen making commercial endorsements, using their high visibility and media identities to sell products, and establishing a star persona specific to, but independent of, the game itself.

As all of America is exposed to commercials, many people who would never watch a basketball game see these basketball star personas, thus extending the league's prominence throughout society and adding to the entertainment aura that surrounds the league. The league's marketing executives have also zeroed in on the presence of Hollywood celebrities at basketball games, using these stars and their love of the game to help sell the entertainment value of the league itself. The Lakers often highlighted the Hollywood celebrities at their games during the 1980s, especially Jack Nicholson, playing up this connection between basketball and Hollywood.

While the league's current status is as a source of entertainment to the masses of American culture, it functions within African American culture on a somewhat different plane. Basketball, along with rap, has come to define contemporary African American cultural production, in terms of aesthetics as well as in terms of masculine articulation.[6] In the era immediately following World War II, however, and certainly through the early part of the 1970s, baseball served as a site for the integration of a Black aesthetic and an early venue for the articulation of a civil rights agenda.

The "breaking of the color line" by Jackie Robinson in 1947 signified a political moment that preceded the highly publicized civil rights movement of Martin Luther King Jr. in the 1960s. Baseball represented one of the oldest bastions of white male dominance in American society. The visible exclusion of African Americans from this "American pastime" was an obvious reminder that Blacks occupied an inferior status relative to whites in America. Robinson's ability to play in the major leagues was as significant a political metaphor for civil rights as any of the other more overtly political events that would define the movement in the 1960s.

Baseball offered the Black males who were finally being allowed to play the game the opportunity to demonstrate their worth as equal American citizens. If sports had any relevance, the superiority of Black baseball players such as Robinson, Satchel Paige, Willie Mays, and Hank Aaron demonstrated that Black athletes, and by extension Black citizens, could be valuable contributors to the progression of America. When Aaron broke what was thought to be an unbreakable record, Babe Ruth's home-run title, in 1974, he ended the reign of metaphoric white supremacy that had dominated the sport. The racial significance of this home run is evidenced by the voluminous racial hate mail that Aaron received on his way to breaking the record. Aaron's historic home run not only demonstrated that the racial discourse about social, cultural, and biological inferiority had no merit, but also proved that given the opportunity, African Americans could excel.

The breaking of the color line in baseball was about proving to white people the inherent value of the African American experience. The game was a proving ground for societal worth and cultural value. Like Cosby, these players were attempting to provide a positive image of Blacks. The problem here comes from attempting to prove to the dominant society one's value on the dominant society's terms. Inevitably, this restrictive scenario forces one to play by a set of rules that are always at the discretion of those in power. In other words, there can never be full acceptance when the manipulative tenets of white supremacy can change the rules at any given time. Thus Blackness, in this construction, is always a product of the white imagination, unable to transform the spaces that it attempts to occupy. Baseball began to lose the cultural significance for the Black masses that it had held at one time.

As the civil rights movement gave way to Black Power, baseball gave way to basketball as a cultural site where the aspirations, the anxieties, and the overall aesthetic of Black culture could be articulated. And though most of today's best baseball players are African American— e.g., Barry Bonds, Frank Thomas, Ken Griffey Jr.—the game itself has fewer Black players overall than in previous generations and maintains less cultural currency in African American culture than ever before.

Baseball has always attempted to maintain tradition at all costs, and the sport seems constantly in a state of nostalgia, referencing its historic, and by extension racist, past. Basketball was ignored in the public imagination for quite some time, and when recognized was perceived only as a sport populated by overpaid Black drug addicts. As a matter of fact, the Lakers' first championship of the Magic Johnson era was played by CBS on tape delay at 11:30 P.M. instead of during prime time, which is now the accepted time slot.

For this reason, basketball was able to create its cultural mythology without the glare of mainstream media attention. Thus its popular history is one of a developing Black aesthetic that came to fruition in the 1980s. Consequently, three-quarters of the players in the league are African American, and the league is now accepted (the presence of Larry Bird notwithstanding) as a Black venue. The celebrated players of past eras are some of the longest-standing popular icons in Black culture. Julius Erving, better known as Dr. J., with his stylish afro, his ever-present knee pads, his leather Converse All-Stars, and his palming of the ABA's colorful red, white, and blue basketball, was one of the most popular images of the 1970s. This image, along with that of a fur coat–wearing, Rolls Royce–driving Walt Frazier, came to represent Black male culture in the 1970s, existing on the same level as the fabled heroes of the Blaxploitation period in Hollywood.

New Jack City

The significant basketball players of the 1970s worked to remove the game from the stale traditions of the textbook and take it into an arena that resembled a sophisticated version of the playground. Many of the jazz musicians of the bebop era took Western culture to task, articulating a distinct Black aesthetic along the way. The players of the 1980s were innovators who took the game to unparalleled heights, working to advance the aesthetic like the purveyors of hard-bop did in the years following bebop.

We now have a new generation of players who have benefited from both traditions, yet are intent on establishing their own image. The new image, though referencing jazz, is consistent with the empowered image and mentality of gangsta rap, or what mainstream culture has most readily identified as "Generation X." The basketball players of this new generation are not only exceptionally gifted, having both knowledge of the game and athletic ability to burn, but they are also blessed with enormous amounts of money and long-term contracts, which offer some sense of freedom. Yet most of these players hail from the same lower-class backgrounds that gangsta rappers detail in their music. The lofty financial status and newfound class distinction embodied by those who come to star in the league are juxtaposed against the lower-class background in which these individuals grew up. Yet the money earned while playing in the NBA dictates a certain freedom which allows them to continue to act in ways normally associated with those who emerge from a marginalized class.

The NBA's "new jacks" are the driving force behind the articulation of the nigga in basketball. With the African American aesthetic having defined the game, it is not unusual that this defiant "don't give a fuck" attitude would dominate the surrounding discourse. And in a sport where race, specifically Blackness, has been normalized through performance, the new issue has become class. This discourse on class can be seen in the recent infusion of Eastern European players who come from war-torn, poverty-stricken environments similar to the racialized American ghetto, from which many of the NBA's Black players emerge. Yet the discourse surrounding class is most evident with regard to the disposition of many of today's young superstars.

Sports Illustrated, in the January 30, 1995, edition, featured an article entitled "Bad Actors: The Growing Number of Selfish and Spoiled Players Are Hurting Their Teams and Marring the NBA's Image"—along with an evocative cover that featured New Jersey Nets star Derrick Coleman with the caption "Waaaaaah!!" (as if to suggest a baby crying) written across his face. The subtitle reads "Petulant Prima Donnas Like New Jersey's Derrick Coleman are Bad News for the NBA."

The accompanying article reveals a certain contempt for the players and their refusal to obey the league's demands, as well as comments which foreground both race and class. The writer, Phil Taylor, begins the article by quoting from Rex Walters, a seldom-used player from the rather pathetic Nets. Walters's comments bemoan the lack of respect that he senses on the part of the players in question. The fact that Walters's opinion is used to justify this scathing article sets him up as one in a position of authority. It is as though he is endowed with the right to pass judgment on those he feels do not live up to his standards, which sound surprisingly close to those of the dominant society, in this case the standards of decorum dictated by the league, but also by most of mainstream white society.

Walters is a white player, and his less than spectacular playing ability highlights his racialized comments even more. Most of the players discussed in the article are African American, who not only have a great deal of playing ability, and in a sense have become stars in the league, but possess the lucrative extended contracts and the nigga's mentality as well. When a seldom-used white player is used to pass judgment on several spectacular Black players, the racial dimension is clearly visible. The NBA is now dominated by African American players, many of whom have benefited from the escalating salaries in professional sports in general and basketball in particular.

For instance, Charlotte's Larry Johnson was awarded an $84 million dollar, 12-year guaranteed contract, ironically announced on the same day as Michael Jordan's announcement that he was retiring from the league. Johnson, at the time in only his third year in the NBA, was given the confidence of financial security that seemingly would erase all of those years growing up in the poverty of a Dallas ghetto. This heightened class status shows in his highly visible gold teeth, which gleam from the camera lighting in the Converse "GrandMaMa" commercials. Whereas the financial aspects of a guaranteed contract indicate entrance into an elite society normally reserved for white males, the gold teeth are a reminder of Johnson's lower-class aesthetic. The gold in his mouth serves as a displacement for real economic power in capitalist America.

Though certain individuals may not wield the financial power signified by the possession of large quantities of gold, it can be held on a much smaller individual scale, albeit in one's mouth, where it is constantly visible as a reminder of a desire to demonstrate economic marginalization. It is for this reason that football superstar Deion Sanders is often seen wearing a large number of gold chains: his heightened class status, achieved from playing football, has given him the wherewithal to purchase what were at one time trinkets, but now are literally pounds of gold. Ultimately, the fact that Johnson has refused to rid himself of the glaring gold teeth while Sanders has resorted to buying bigger and better gold suggests that though both individuals are now in a financial category that would normally suggest elite status, they choose to retain their lower-class visual aesthetic so as to defiantly reject the accepted decorum of their recently acquired class position.

An interesting contrast to this common image of defiance in the modern game of basketball is the elusive image of Dennis Rodman. Rodman constantly challenges the boundaries of Black masculinity. On the cover of the May 29, 1995, *Sports Illustrated*, he is pictured with flaming reddish-orange hair, a dog collar, several earrings in both his ears and nose, a sleeveless vest which resembles a halter top, and a pair of iridescent hot pants. In the photo layout that accompanies the article, we see him in a leather vest sprawled across a couch, with his navel ring clearly in view.

Rodman—who is known for his unpredictable behavior, which has included missing practices, avoiding team huddles, and removing his shoes while the game is in progress—in these photos openly pushes the boundaries of masculinity, particularly in light of the ultramasculine ethos that dominates the NBA and male sports in general. Rodman also defies the traditional expression of Black male style in regard to both performance and dress.

Rodman's embrace of the signs of gay culture and sadomasochism in his dress is in clear contrast to the sartorial elegance normally associated with professional ballplayers. Rodman openly states his interest in gay sexuality and brings a critique to bear on the extremes of masculinity, of which the playing of sports is the epitome in our heterosexual-dominated society. On the other hand, his open defiance of league rules and protocol places him squarely in the middle of the debate surrounding the nigga mentality and the NBA. Rodman can be said to exhibit the same gender-bending sexuality as pop music star Prince. Yet Prince's extravagance is less spectacular within the music industry, where excess and rejection of the accepted codes of masculinity are less rare. On the other hand, as Rodman declares in the *SI* article, "I'm not an athlete anymore. I'm an entertainer" (Silver, 22). His appearance and his antics have allowed him to transcend the narrow confines of masculinity according to basketball and enter the world of entertainment in the broadest sense, redefining the codes of sexuality and class along the way.[7]

Derrick Coleman, who, like Johnson, has a long-term guaranteed contract worth in excess of $70 million, is the main target of criticism in the *Sports Illustrated* piece. In 1993 Coleman bought the lower-class house that he grew up in on Detroit's embittered North End, then set about renovating it, as it, like many of the homes in the neighborhood, had become dilapidated over the years. The purchase of this house for his personal use suggests that Coleman still embraces the lower-class environment in which he grew up, though his current class status places him among the financial elite.

It is this lower-class embrace that seems to fuel Coleman's defiant attitude toward established authority. The *Sports Illustrated* story relates an incident between Coleman and his coach Butch Beard, who happens to be African American also. Beard had instituted a team policy which required players to wear a coat and tie when traveling. Coleman refused to cooperate. Beard suggested to Coleman that if he did not comply, he would be fined until he did. Coleman responded by giving Beard a blank check.

This gesture signifies on multiple levels. Not only is Coleman refusing to adopt the attire that he associates with mainstream society, he is also saying that because of his superior class status, the fines that Beard intends to levy against him cannot affect him enough to make him agree to cooperate, as he has so much money that the fines could not possibly have any impact. The fact that Beard is also African American, occupying a certain place of authority and power as coach, has no effect on Coleman's judgment; he sees Beard as simply a pawn in the larger scheme of things relative to the NBA. The fact that Coleman's salary far exceeds that of his coach makes it quite difficult for the latter to exert his usual power and control. Beard then possesses power only in a metaphorical sense, but when he attempts to enforce this power, he realizes that he is dealing in the imaginary, while Coleman exists in the real.

In college, by contrast, coaches are given long-term contracts, shoe deals, and television programs, yet their power tends to go unquestioned. Incidentally, most of the coaches at the most visible college programs are white, while in the NBA the players—those who are asserting this sort of power from the positions of workers, if you will—are primarily African American.

This reversal of power is interesting with respect to race and class, yet it is difficult to talk about "workers" in any traditional sense in light of the amount of money made by a player such as Coleman. The racial and class overtones become increasingly apparent upon further investigation. Orlando Magic general manger Pat Williams describes the current situation as consistent with Republican rhetoric on the declining family values in society, specifically in Black America. Williams states that "young people are less tolerant of authority than they were 10, 20 years ago, and some of that can be traced back to the breakdown of the traditional family unit" (23).

This widely held view is in line with the sentiments that foster a fear of lower-class African American male assertion in society. In addition to Williams and this conservative sentiment, several of the league's older, more established stars have voiced their concern about the deteriorating state of the game due to the selfish identity associated with the new generation. Players such as Charles Barkley and Karl Malone have publicly commented on their disapproval of the NBA's new jacks.

Barkley, who seems to exhibit the behavior of the nigga when convenient, argued that if many of the game's younger players were not playing basketball, they would be gang members. Malone, on the other hand, was recently chided by Coleman—clearly demonstrating that Coleman has little regard for his elders—for being an "Uncle Tom," which forced Malone to begin defensively explaining his companionship with many white friends. Even Magic Johnson, who for a brief period late in the 1993–94 season coached his former team, the Lakers, publicly stated that the players' obsession with the material benefits of playing in the NBA has detracted from their ability to play basketball. These misplaced priorities are supposedly what led Magic to end his short-lived coaching career after only a small number of games.

This contempt on the part of an older generation, and lack of respect from the new players, is not surprising. The members of an older generation always resent the benefits given to the younger generation, which they often feel have come at their expense. It also seems that the older players have a legitimate gripe in consideration of the fact that the salaries given to many of the younger players far outdistance those of their older counterparts, though many of these young players have yet to equal the production of their predecessors.

The conflict in this situation seems to lie in the individual's embrace of power over the interest of the team in what is clearly a team sport. Thus players such as Coleman seem selfish in placing their interests first. However, because the players are still pawns of the individual team owners, who are seldom criticized for their use of power, and of the larger structure of the league, to be cut or traded without any voice in the decision, this financial freedom offers Black men some (albeit limited) sense of power in a world where real power is not easy to come by. The league and the corporate forces that sponsor the NBA have created a series of monsters which have come back to haunt them.

The articulation of Black male identity from a perspective that resembles the threatening posture of the nigga seems to have pervaded the NBA and, like gangsta rap, has bridged the gap between cultural production from a Black aesthetic and widespread acceptance from a mass audience along the way. These Black players who embrace the nigga persona have embraced the mainstream and transformed it, without being fully compromised by it.

Yet this generational difference, though important, pales beside the issue of class status, which has recently taken over the league's discourse about reclaiming its image, especially as it relates to the figure of 1994–95 NBA co–rookie of the year Grant Hill. Hill brings an upper-class discourse to bear on a league permeated by the ethos of lower-class politics. Hill's pedigree distinguishes him from many of his NBA peers. His father, Calvin Hill, a Yale graduate, was a running back for the 1972 Super Bowl champion Dallas Cowboys and most recently an executive board member of the Baltimore Orioles, while Grant's mother, Janet, was a roommate of Hillary Rodham Clinton at Wellesley and is now a partner in a Washington, D.C., consulting firm with former secretary of the Navy Clifford Alexander. Grant's background reflects not only a certain economic stability and class status, but also a significant amount of power when juxtaposed with the impoverished single-parent household typical of many of the league's other players.

In addition, Grant himself graduated from Duke, having starred on a team which, though successful, seldom recruits or features Black players in prominent roles. The university's elite southern reputation also works to enforce an image of a privileged class when contrasted to the basketball factories that most successful college programs have become. Thus Grant Hill's presence in the league creates a viable alternative to the "bootstraps" discourse articulated in *Hoop Dreams*, which suggests that the NBA is a potential means of escape from the lifelong association with poverty that most of the underclass and the players who come from this background now inhabit. His class-based behavior is now celebrated by those who see the truly disadvantaged as a constant reminder of America's refusal to deal with the issues of race and class.

With the increasing disdain for the new generation of ballplayers, Hill seems a welcome savior for those concerned with maintaining a positive image, and class becomes the key component in this quest. Hill appears on the cover of the April 1995 *GQ* with the rather dubious question "Can Grant Hill Save Sports?" The real question becomes, Save sports from what? The article opens by detailing Hill's appearance at a party thrown by one of his teammates, Terry Mills, in downtown Detroit. The writer, Tom Junod, describes the scene as full of "hoodlums," with the exception of Hill, whom he constantly refers to as being out of place. Junod details the scene: "There were these guys in these long mink coats, wearing these big mink hats, and you just know they had guns stuffed in their pockets. There were these crazy women running around, who were with the hoodlums but who were all drunk and lubricious, and ready to go. And in the middle of this chaos was none other than Grant Hill" (170).

This description sets forth the class politics that define Hill's present circumstances. With the public impression of Detroit as the embodiment of the postindustrial in America, the underworld drug economy also being implied here, the description of hoodlums finds its emphasis in the race and class politics of contemporary urban America. The fact that the Pistons, Detroit's team, really play in suburban Auburn Hills contributes to the contrast between inner-city Detroit and the bucolic suburbs. Hill, who is clearly defined as a suburban subject, appears out of place with the racially specific class politics that define the party. Drugs, guns, and sexually loose women are assumed to be part of the landscape inhabited by the truly disadvantaged of America, and this landscape is associated with many of the players in the NBA—except Hill, of course.

Considering that a large percentage of the league's players are Black, the racial politics speak for themselves. This allows for the class-specific politics that circulate around Hill. Since it is difficult to make an argument against race as being problematic in the NBA, being that Blackness has clearly made the league successful, a distorted class aesthetic becomes the distinctive characteristic. With so few Black players coming from elite backgrounds, a player such as Hill stands out as an object of desire. His class status is seen both as novel and as emblematic of the league's desired image, one of entertainment with "class," even though class in this case happens to be encased in Black. Hill's image has come to resemble that of a modern-day Cosby, or better yet, the descendant and beneficiary of that upper-class Black tradition. Thus several commentators, including Junod in the GQ piece, celebrate Hill's skill at playing the piano, when it is assumed that most of his peers have no musical inclinations, other than the specifically lower-class admiration for what is openly thought of as the unmusical dimension of rap music.

Yet there is a dark underside to this class valorization. To highlight Hill's elite class status is to assume that Blackness and lower-class existence are fundamental to each other, that Hill has somehow transcended his race via his elite economic and social background. The cover of GQ pictures a smiling Hill dressed in a fashionable suit and tie, making a basketball pass through his legs. With GQ having established itself as a magazine of style for the modern man, this picture stands in stark contrast to the usual cover photo. GQ is known for its images of cool and distinctive style, with the figures on the cover dressed in the latest fashions to highlight their sense of style and current popularity.

Hill is shown smiling and playing basketball, though dressed in a stylish linen suit, while football superstar Joe Montana is simply pictured in a stationary photo that highlights his suede jacket. It is as though the Black man cannot be separated from the sport that has made him famous, but also acceptable. It appears that the magazine, and by extension society, is comfortable with Grant Hill the educated basketball player, but not Grant Hill the educated, articulate Black man whose image stands on its own, like Montana, above and beyond his sport, based on the ability to foreground a substantial image of masculinity.

Basketball, like music, has established itself as a cultural venue heavy on history and substance. As we can always gauge what is happening in the larger African American population by the latest musical trends, we must come to recognize the significant contributions of sport to the evolving body of work on Blackness. The class warfare that currently divides the league over its public image is the same class warfare that currently divides Black America.

Much as is happening in the NBA, African American society experiences internal difficulties because of its refusal to acknowledge the demands of its lower-class citizens. This image problem must be addressed before there can be any real progress with respect to the future power base that will define the world in which both sets live. As with the fusing of the formal and the vernacular, the collective power of combining lower-class and elite-class positions remains fundamental to future elevation that will supersede individual tokenism for group access to the corridors of power.

Epilogue: Some New, Improved Shit

I don't want nobody to give me nothing
Just open up the door
I'll get it myself.
—James Brown, "I Don't Want Nobody to Give Me Nothing"

Fuck the world
Don't ask me for shit
Everything you get
You gotta work hard for it.
—The Notorious B.I.G. and Method Man, "The What"

Multiple tensions define the contemporary cultural expression of the truly disadvantaged Black male. Forwarding a defiant posture that eschews mainstream accommodation but is continually consumed by the mainstream suggests something at work that defies normal cultural representation.

In many ways, this contemporary situation is akin to the dilemma faced by John Hull, Lawrence Fishburne's character in *Deep Cover*. Hull, also known as Russell Stevens, is an undercover narcotics officer who is constantly shifting identities in a sting operation that not only compromises his initially naive reasons for joining the force—to help his people—but also eventually forces him into a life of crime, though it is justified by the law. The film reveals both government and police complicity in the drug trade, foregrounding the contradictory rhetoric that has surrounded this situation since the Reagan/Bush era. At the film's conclusion, Hull has come into possession of a large sum of money which he has obtained illegally through his masquerade as a drug dealer. He ponders, in voiceover, his possible options:

> We took 11 million in profits out of the van. The money doesn't know where it came from, but I do. If I keep it, I'm a criminal. If I give it to the government, I'm a fool. If I try and do some good with it, maybe it just makes things worse. Either way I'll probably just wind up getting myself in more trouble. It's an impossible chore, but in a way, we all have to make it. What would you do?

Hull's question is a direct challenge to the producers of Black popular culture. It is also a challenge to Black people in America today regarding their general state of cynicism and apathy. With the civil rights movement having resulted in middle-class selfishness, accommodation, and isolation from the larger community of Black people, and with the attempts on the part of the right to reverse the few individual gains made during our time, there are few real choices left. As Black America—and America in general, for that matter, faces a lack of competent, committed, and sincere leadership, and the feeling that there is nothing to "look forward to," we as individuals are pushed into a difficult corner that makes self-aggrandizement, or "gettin' paid," seem to be the only logical and satisfying conclusion.

These trends help to define the cultural representations of the truly disadvantaged and their presence in popular culture. How many contemporary athletes would endure the sacrifice rendered by Muhammad Ali, to willingly forgo the fame and financial stability that goes along with his profession to stand up for a social and political issue? Not only are contemporary athletes apolitical, but they have no real cause to stand up for if they wanted to. This is not intended as uninformed nostalgia, but as descriptive of a situation where cynicism and willing compromise pervade popular culture and our daily lives.

The problems faced by players in the NBA with respect to attitude, financial freedom, and their place in society are complicated at levels that normally go undiscussed. In light of how our society pampers young male athletes with a potential for success and how this pampering often confounds serious problems of socialization that tend to be ignored, the resulting pathologies—alcohol and drug abuse, spousal abuse, financial mismanagement, etc.—should come as no surprise. When you attempt to ease the problems of the truly disadvantaged by ignoring them and then covering them up with money, you are in essence putting Band-Aids™ on bullet wounds. In a way, you are making these men hurt themselves.

Removing individuals from their truly disadvantaged backgrounds, in most cases overnight, and placing them in opulence through million-dollar contracts, without addressing their social and cultural needs, often makes matters worse instead of better. The sharp contrast between the ghetto and the life of a millionaire can easily cause "a fool and his money" to "soon part." These individuals tend to live in isolated bubbles which will probably burst at some point in their life. When this happens as a result of age, declining skills, or both, they rarely have the social and cultural skills to deal with life in the "real" world. The money can greatly enhance their lives—at least this is the illusion—or it can compound their problems by giving them the freedom to do whatever their newfound wealth will allow, without teaching them the true realities of everyday life.

This is true not just in basketball, as such problems have befallen popular Black athletes in other sports as well. It is also not exclusive to the current generation of players, as both Joe Louis and Jesse Owens died paupers. But with the enormous amounts of money now available to professional athletes, one would assume that there would be differences. Among the most notable riches-to-rags stories are those of baseball's Darryl Strawberry and Dwight Gooden, and football's Lawrence Taylor. White ballplayers, like white men in society, seem to have a separate set of rules, as baseball pitcher Steve Howe has demonstrated time and time again. A repeat drug offender, he has never faced the sanctions that his Black counterparts have. It is important to add that many Black athletes are not satisfied with being the victims of addiction and social pathology and use their rehabilitation to reformulate their life's mission; witness the heroic return of former basketball player turned coach and administrator John Lucas.

A most compelling recent case is that of troubled boxer Mike Tyson. Tyson's prowess as a boxer rejuvenated interest in the floundering heavyweight boxing division, yet his public mishaps have generated as much, if not more, publicity.

Tyson's biography is well known, having been presented regularly on the nightly news and in several sports profiles. The most popular discussions of his life have been Barbara Kopple's *Fallen Champ*, originally broadcast on NBC in early 1993, and HBO's original movie *Tyson*, a fictionalized account of the boxer's life originally broadcast in the spring of 1995, shortly after Tyson's release from prison.

Both films, most notably the Kopple documentary, show how Tyson's early childhood upbringing in Brooklyn was marred by trouble with the law, mostly having to do with crimes of a violent nature. Yet these problems not only were not addressed, they were exploited. Cus D'Amato, Tyson's mentor and adopted father figure, has been credited by many with saving Tyson's life, yet the documentary reveals that D'Amato overlooked Tyson's problems and was responsible for channeling his rage into boxing. While this would seem a good way of dealing with his violent temperament, D'Amato never attempted to educate the young Tyson in the ways of the world, nor did he socialize this uncontrollable brute. Instead he taught Tyson that his boxing skills were all that mattered, and this emphasis on violence inadvertently created and nurtured a sanctioned killer. The rage with which Tyson dominated the ring was a choreographed version of the same rage that defined his relationships with women and all others who got in his way.

To make matters worse, everyone who came in contact with Tyson, even after D'Amato, attempted to exploit him as well. This includes managers Jim Jacobs and Bill Cayton, his divorced wife Robin Givens, and his current manager, Don King. Thus Tyson's boxing skills proved profitable for everyone involved, except, of course, Tyson himself. Tyson's ultimate arrest on rape charges, which many still do not accept, was more an accident waiting to happen than it was a surprise or, worse, a planned conspiracy, as some misguided supporters would argue. Even though Tyson's rape of Desiree Washington may appear suspect, I have always viewed the conviction as the chickens coming home to roost, much like Tupac's rape conviction, wherein past deeds of sexual abuse and violence toward women which were never reported came back to haunt him in the worst way.

Yet even after Tyson had served a three-year prison term, his highly publicized release from incarceration demonstrated some of the same potential problems arising again. Tyson was immediately given a multi-million-dollar contract from the Showtime network for exclusive rights to his future fights, and he was celebrated in many circles of the African American community as some sort of hero. This seems to reward his time in jail as opposed to allowing him to slowly be rehabilitated back into society. It is as though he got a delayed bonus for going to jail, instead of any real punishment.

Though countless numbers of young Black men have disappeared in America's prejudiced penal system—some guilty, others astoundingly innocent—Tyson's situation does not help matters. As long as Tyson is profitable to others, be they boxing promoters or cable networks, he will be compensated, his violent disposition rewarded, regardless of his social problems outside the boxing ring.

As a community, though, we must not embrace these obviously wayward people just on the basis of their race; nor can we be quick to judge the downfall of one individual as representative of the race, as self-hatred would have us do. To embrace Tyson as a hero points to the problematic dearth of real Black icons worthy of such honor, and to use his problems as representative of the race is a clear demonstration of racism and its effects. Instead we must recognize that systemic racism can have multiple facets, and adding to an already lost cause can be one of them.

Of course, my explanation of Tyson's situation should in no way be taken as a justification of his behavior. Spousal abuse and rape are unacceptable under any circumstances. I am simply pointing out that Tyson is as much a victim as he is a perpetrator, and the profit-motivated system that allows this has complicated matters more for truly disadvantaged Black men than it has assisted them. As long as the hierarchical inequities persist with respect to ownership, corporate sponsorship, network contracts, and other aspects of financial interest along the way, truly disadvantaged Black males will be exploited by a system, as *Hoop Dreams* so accurately points out, that many feel is their only means of possible liberation.

Similar cultural contradictions at work in music and cinema. Take, for instance, the case of Time Warner, one of the largest corporate media conglomerates in the entertainment industry, which is constantly subjected to criticism from conservative groups about the gangsta rap sold under some of its record labels.

On one hand, Time Warner represents the epitome of corporate capitalism and in many ways, through its actions, is an obvious supporter of conservative ideology. On the other hand, the corporation makes a great deal of money off of the controversial music in question and thus is forced to defend the artists to make this profit possible. As long as gangsta rap proves profitable, some opportunistic company, if not Time Warner, will market the material. The dictates of the marketplace are such that mainstream corporations do not mind going against the conservative principles that uphold their existence.

Thus, when conservative critics of gangsta rap such as William Bennett, Newt Gingrich, and Bob Dole link the genre with the excessive rate of violence in America and American popular culture, they should really focus their misguided frustration on companies such as Time Warner, which their conservative thoughts and political action most directly benefit. They should also take a look at the history of media representation and recognize that their celebrated political mentor, Ronald Reagan, used the violent characterizations of Rambo and Dirty Harry to support his own militarily aggressive posture only a short time ago. This conservative embrace of violent aggression is seldom challenged on the same level as are gangsta rappers, but the results seem to be much more devastating. The same entertainment structure that made John Wayne, Clint Eastwood, Sylvester Stallone, and Arnold Schwarzenegger heroes based on their prowess at violent aggression helped make Ice Cube, Dr. Dre, Snoop Doggy Dogg, and Tupac Shakur best-selling musical acts. So why is one group guilty of destroying society and the other group simply heroic? This same contradictory attitude toward violence has led to the rise of the various militia groups around the country who see the use of violence against their own government as an acceptable form of expression.

African American cultural producers have begun to resort to the same tactics that have long defined white male articulation in culture, violence and aggression, as a way of maintaining their cultural presence and increasing their own financial viability at the same time. It should not be a surprise that these sentiments are being expressed as they are. When your existence in America begins with the violence of the slave trade and each subsequent generation is forced to deal with the legacy of this violence in one form or another, it is inevitable that the continued violent oppression of your daily life, be it physical, economic, or mental, if not all three, will be expressed as violence. When mainstream media institutions realize that this rage is profitable and discover that its expression is the path to success, these violent tendencies start to become the rule rather than the exception.

These African American performers must share some of the blame, as there can be no justification for the excessive violence in many underclass Black communities and the relationship between it and gangsta rap and gangsta imagery. However, the ultimate problem is not the violence that the gangsta represents, for these tales from the 'hood are often much-needed, sophisticated, personalized looks into a world that would otherwise get no mainstream exposure. Instead, the problem has to do with a denial of access to the power of representation in anything but token ways. These narratives of life in the 'hood could be augmented well by similarly poignant stories about other aspects of Black life.

Music is always a good barometer of Black life. Popular music today reveals that Black people are living some very foul lives. Through years of oppression, racism has finally had its most significant internal impact. Many in the truly disadvantaged community now celebrate the very things that keep them enslaved. This is not necessarily new, yet the presentation of it in the media by African Americans makes it an interesting topic of discussion.

Bones, Thug, N' Harmony's single "Da 1st of tha Month" celebrates the day when people get their government assistance allotment. The cover of Ol Dirty Bastard's album *Return of the 36 Chambers* prominently features his real welfare identification card. While some may see this as humorous, the acceptance and celebration of being on welfare is far from funny. The point at which people openly begin to endorse this lifestyle is the point at which we stop laughing to keep from crying, and instead cry to admit our true feelings and our true state of depravity. As Carter G. Woodson said some time ago, "When you control a man's thinking you do not have to worry about his actions. You do not have to tell him to stand here or go yonder. He will find his proper place and will stay in it. You do not need to send him to the back door. He will go without being told. In fact, if there is no back door, he will cut one for his special benefit" (xiii). This prophetic line explains why racism throughout the history of America has resulted in ideas such as those promoted by Bones, Thug, N' Harmony and Ol Dirty Bastard. This represents a problem of epic proportions.

The other major difficulty in dealing with the gangsta genre is its rather limited view of life outside the 'hood. For instance, crime has helped to propel several other ethnic groups into "legitimate" business—this is what Coppola deals with in the *Godfather* films—yet African Americans seem not to recognize the temporary nature of this enterprise. Indeed, many seem to want to make a career out of it. While I recognize the social factors that distinguish white from African American ethics, it is time to go legitimate. To limit your experiences to a single space of existence, in this case a perpetual underworld economy, is problematic. True advancement comes only from exposing yourself to the world and all its possibilities, both physically and metaphorically.

The 'hood is too narrow a frame of reference, too small a sample to draw from. The 'hood is only a section in a much larger city, state, country, and world. To exist in the coming century, it will be necessary to coexist with the world, and not simply to exist in the 'hood. It is past time for advancement as a group, and though I strongly acknowledge the difficulties of progress in a society dead set against you, we must realize that these situations will not change without some individual initiative. This initiative involves upgrading our point of reference to encompass the global 'hood and all the requirements of citizenship that go along with membership in this redefined group. This cannot happen by remaining in the 'hood, though a working knowledge of the 'hood is fundamental to any future success, just as a working knowledge of the blues is paramount to any cultural articulation. The 'hood must be a point of transcendence, a stepping stone to the future.

Some recent examples of gangsta rap demonstrate a subtle move away from the redundant celebration of violence, aggression, and confrontation. Some of the most popular rappers have begun to analyze their own articulation by removing themselves from the fray, so as to provide an insider's view of the impact these forms have had. Ice Cube has evolved in each of his projects, highlighted by the self-reflexive "It Was a Good Day." Other hard-core rappers have begun to do the same at an even more personal level. Most notable are Scarface, Snoop Doggy Dogg, Tupac, and The Notorious B.I.G. (aka Biggie Smalls).

Snoop's powerful "Murder Was the Case" is a depressing tale of a gangsta's demise when given one more chance to redeem himself from the murderous life he has led, yet he fails even at the second chance. It is as though the life of a gangsta is an endless cycle that the perpetrator is destined to remain caught up in—in other words, "crime don't pay." Scarface's "Never Seen a Man Cry" tells a similar story about a young man's first murder and his eventual descent into hell, both figuratively and literally. Once again, the self-reflexive impulse tells the listener, in so many words, that "crime don't pay," a far cry from advocating crime as a way of life.

Tupac Shakur was also involved in a renegotiation of gangsta rap on the album *Me against the World* (1995), but returned to straight-up gansta rap on his last album, *All Eyez on Me* (1996). On *Me against the World*, Tupac continually refers to himself as a victim in search of help, which no one would give him when he needed it, while at the same time he confesses his propensity toward violent behavior and asks for forgiveness. The first single, "Dear Mama," is a tribute to his mother, but also a public apology for the unnecessary worries that he has caused her through the years. The album is also an after-the-fact prophecy—"Who'd known in elementary / That I'd see the penitentiary?"—as he can see his own demise, but looks to warn others following the same path. *Me against the World* is a desperate man's cry for help, an apology for past sins, but most important of all, it is a revision on the unapologetic gangsta genre.

Scarface was originally a member of the Geto Boys and helped write the now-legendary song "Mind Playing Tricks on Me," one of the first significant self-reflexive delvings into the psyche of the gangsta and the paranoia that accompanies life in the 'hood. Scarface's statement that he is "having fatal thoughts of suicide" provoked the exploration of suicide as an answer to the problems of a troubled existence by The

Notorious B.I.G. on his evocatively titled debut album, *Ready to Die* (1994). B.I.G. not only thinks about suicide but has one track, "Suicidal Thoughts," devoted to his self-indulgent fantasy of taking his own life as a way of settling the score.

What is startling about these fantasies is that suicide has never been prevalent in the Black community. African Americans have long regarded their suffering and resilience as a badge of honor. In the mentality of the gangsta community, suicide is not even a consideration, as the violent lifestyle they lead will surely result in their own death while in pursuit of their nihilistic life. To die in a hail of bullets is not only exciting, but, as Bishop in *Juice* constantly informs us, it is even honorable. Thus suicide is considered cowardly and a violation of the codes of hardened masculinity.

Yet by the time we get to B.I.G's debut, suicide has not only become an option, it is a considered reality, as the covert suicidal mission that defines the gangsta lifestyle seems to have played out. It is no longer glamorous to shield oneself against the troubles of the world by hiding underground in the gangsta life while the world outside is closing in; it has now become acceptable at least to consider suicide as a way to escape a world too difficult to navigate. B.I.G.'s fantasy puts us in touch with the depressed state of contemporary life in the 'hood.

As one of the most popular and respected new rappers on the scene, B.I.G. seems interested in transforming and expanding gangsta rap. His first single off the *Ready to Die* album, "Juicy," exemplifies this fully. Rap, for Biggie Smalls, is about the whole range of emotions that define contemporary Black male life. In "Juicy," rap becomes a means of social mobility: "Now I'm in the limelight / Cause I rhyme tight / Time to get paid / Blow up like the World Trade." Thus his skills are his ticket out of the ghetto. Biggie celebrates his newfound class ascendancy with pleasure: "Fifty-inch screen / Money green leather sofa / Got two cars / A limousine / With a chauffeur / Phone bill about two 'g's flat / No need to worry / My accountant handles that / And my whole crew is lounging / Celebratin' every day / No more public housing."

If nothing else, this track seems to indicate that some rappers are no longer content with dwelling in the ghetto forever; instead they strive for upward mobility, informed by but transcended like the gangsta ethos of legitimacy mentioned earlier with the *Godfather* films. The life of poverty is no longer seen as a badge of honor, nor as a sign of one's hardness. Instead, this unfortunate life is to be discarded as soon as possible. "We used to fuss when the landlord dissed us / No heat / Wonder why Christmas / Missed us / Birthdays was the worst days / Now we sip champagne when we thirsty."

In addition to its potential for class mobility, and thus its importance as a determinant social factor, rap serves historical functions as well. The introduction to Biggie's album begins with the sounds of a mother giving birth, and as the sounds of labor fill the air, we hear the music of Curtis Mayfield from the soundtrack of *Superfly*.

This tune not only links this modern-day project with the historical, but also defines Biggie's position in life. The masterful work of Curtis Mayfield on this soundtrack deals with the film's main character, and by extension all of Black America, in a collective upward class movement. As the song echoes its recurrent chorus, "tryin' to get over," the necessity of daily struggle, due to the limitations of racism and class subordination, becomes increasingly clear. The fact that this tune is linked so closely to Biggie's entrance into the world suggests that his life will be one of constant struggle.

As the sounds of Mayfield die out, we hear an argument between Biggie's parents about the child's incorrigible behavior. Each parent blames the other for the child's early flirtation with criminal activity. The music we hear is the Sugar Hill Gang rap classic "Rapper's Delight," the song many credit with being the beginning of rap on a popular scale. Here Biggie's adolescence is linked with the emerging history of the rap form, with specific attention to how rap will come to define this generation of African American youth.

When the screams of parents and Sugar Hill are no longer audible, we begin to hear the full-throated bass voice belonging to a newly developed menace to society in the form of Biggie Smalls. The music is that of Audio Two, and the tune is "Top Billing." With the year being 1987, we are firmly into the second half of the most deadly decade for Black Americans in the twentieth century. As Ronald Reagan gives way to George Bush, we realize that Biggie is now a product of his own mediated environment, and like Priest in *Superfly* and a number of other brothers before him, he has chosen the road of least resistance, a full-on criminal lifestyle. Here he is heard cajoling a partner in crime to help him rob a subway train. As they go to get on the train, Biggie queries his somewhat frightened friend, "Nigga, this is 1987; is you dead broke?" Thus this year, 1987—incidentally the same year people were seeing the presentation of wealth in the fictional Oliver Stone film *Wall Street* and trying to recover from the financial crash of the real Wall Street—ties into the dismal financial circumstances of disenfranchised Black youth in America.

The familiar musings of Snoop Doggy Dogg, in his standout freestyle "Tha Shiznit," signal that we are now in the present. Snoop is the obvious selection as a purveyor of artistic and cultural excellence, and his close proximity to the plight of the truly disadvantaged Black male makes him an appropriate reference point for cultural credibility. We also hear a conversation between Biggie and a prison guard. The guard suggests to Biggie that he will be back soon, but Biggie responds by saying, "You won't be seeing me up in this motherfucker," and goes on to tell him that he has "big plans," which are obviously related to his rap career.

This introduction is significant in that it uses music, particularly rap, as a vehicle for the expression of personal history. The fact that Biggie's own narrative is so closely aligned with the growth of rap demonstrates that rap itself has become the cultural forum for an entire generation, as well as a significant means of expression for the young Black male. Rap is the music of the disenfranchised, but more important, it has now become a vehicle for movement from lower-class life into middle-class existence, in much the same way that successful Black athletes enter a new, plush lifestyle as they move from college to the professional ranks.

For Biggie, rap parallels his own move from the slavery of ghetto life to the perceived freedom of middle-class existence. The line "Remember Rappin' Duke / Da ha, da ha / You never thought that hip-hop would make it this far" confronts the critics who suggested that rap was a passing fad. This same sort of criticism assumed that Biggie would fall victim to the streets, as opposed to taking these experiences and using them as material for his upward social climb: "I'm blowin' up like I said I would / Call the crib / Same number / Same 'hood / It's all good." The denigration of rap is linked with the personal denigration that Biggie felt growing up, yet the success of his musical endeavors, like the popular success of rap, is further evidence that Biggie and rap have blown up, against all odds, right alongside each other.

This passage of gangsta rap out of the oppressive conditions of the ghetto, its use as a vehicle for middle-class mobility, not only is surprising, considering the hard posture of nonconformity associated with it, but also confounds those who have suggested that the genre is dead. Instead of dying off, the music reinvents itself by recognizing the benefits of a so-called normal existence, and by maintaining the hard edge in perspective that has been its foundation.

The soundtrack has proven to be a new means of expanding the influence of this musical genre. Dr. Dre's production of the soundtracks for *Murder Was the Case* and *Above the Rim,* both in 1994, continued to develop a space for the proliferation of the music. Both albums demonstrate the influence that gangsta rap has had on R & B, with singers such as Nate Dogg and Jewell, using the lyrical styling of gangsta rap and vocal inflection normally associated with gospel, and linking these with the more traditional R & B sound. Not only has the music expanded, it has also demonstrated its influence on other musical genres, a true testament to its strength. Director F. Gary Gray's smash hit film *Friday* (1995), which resonates with the style of the most extreme elements of Black folk culture—once called the "chitlin circuit"—stars Ice Cube. This comedy is directly influenced by gangsta rap, which demonstrates the transferal of the gangsta ethos to another media form. The humor in the film is reminiscent of Rudy Ray Moore, Leroy and Skillet, and LaWanda Page, popular Black folk comics from the 1970s. For the time being, the gangsta genre seems alive and well, as it diversifies into other media forms.

Culture is a small but powerful vessel in a much larger fleet of societal components. When specific to African American culture, the dynamics become even more intricate, though constantly expansive. The most oppressed people in any given society will undoubtedly bring a significant difference to bear on the culture that they are allowed to produce. This production is never any more or any less than what their lived experiences dictate to them.

The strength, though, comes in the articulation. Black men have always had a different take on the world. Even Clarence Thomas's brand of political conservatism is specific to his truly disadvantaged childhood and his navigation of the world since that time. This distinct style of the truly disadvantaged Black male is not new, but the currents that have forced a response are. Thus the resulting cultural products are representative of the situation. When we listen to the phat beats of the latest gangsta rap tunes or witness the grace and determination with which certain ballplayers float through the air, and note not only how much money these movements are worth but how these events can be seen to define certain aspects of America, we are witnessing the magic of what it means to be a Black man in America. When we read about another "gang-related" shooting or the squandering of another million by a star athlete, we are witnessing the underside of this magic. Magic, here, is transformed into voodoo. When we combine the two sides, maybe we can begin to understand the impact that America has on Black men and the impact that Black men have on America.

Notes

Real Niggaz Don't Die

1. These critical tensions, which came in the form of both public debate and private conversation, inform Sut Jhally and Justin Lewis's *Enlightened Racism: The Cosby Show, Audiences, and the Myth of the American Dream,* a book which analyzes the various discursive arguments that circulated about the program. As a matter of fact, Bill Cosby himself financed the research for the book.

2. For a detailed discussion of the word "nigger" in popular culture, see my articles "Tarantino's Mantra?" about filmmaker Quentin Tarantino's use of the word in his films, and "The Day the Niggaz Took Over."

3. See my article "The Meaning of the Blues" for a discussion of how this concept works in contemporary culture.

Check Yo Self Before You Wreck Yo Self

1. Texts devoted to analyzing rap music and contemporary culture have been appearing with increasing regularity, especially in light of past omissions. For instance, academic texts such as Houston Baker Jr.'s *Rap Music, Black Studies, and the Academy,* Tricia Rose's book *Black Noise: Rap Music and Black Culture in Contemporary America,* and a large segment of Gina Dent's edited volume *Black Popular Culture* are devoted to the subject. In addition, Nelson George, whose work on rap is largely chronicled in *Buppies, B-Boys, BAPS, and Bohos,* and Greg Tate, author of *Flyboy in the Buttermilk,* both former *Village Voice* writers, have gained increased attention as authorities in this regard. The popularity of magazines such as *The Source* and *Vibe* adds to this recent phenomenon.

2. For an extended explanation of the "death of politics" relative to popular culture, see my analysis of Spike Lee's *Malcolm X,* "Popular Culture and Political Empowerment," in the *Cineaste* critical symposium on the same subject.

3. In addition to female rappers such as Salt n Pepa, Queen Latifah, and MC Lyte, whom Rose discusses extensively in her book *Black Noise,* the emergence of West Coast gangsta rap, which is absent from Rose's analysis, does not directly address women rappers such as Yo Yo and Boss, who offer interesting possibilities for the continued exploration of gender issues in rap music. I will devote specific attention to Boss in chapter 3.

4. The following West Coast rappers exemplify thematically my argument for Black male angst: Snoop Doggy Dog, Ice-T, the late Easy E, Niggas Wit Attitude (NWA), Compton's Most Wanted (CMW), Tha Dogg Pound, Dr. Dre, King Tee, 2 Pac, Paris, Too Short, Warren G, Coolio, Mack 10, and most notably Ice Cube.

5. As an example, De La's first single, "Me, Myself, and I," critiqued how many rappers assume a monolithic posture instead of being themselves. Thus, they rejected the b-boy style of wearing gold chains, Kangol caps, and lambskin coats for their own stylized attire of uncombed hair and nondescript baggy clothes. As the title, "Me, Myself, and I," states, they were concerned with asserting their own identity, while simultaneously offering a plural definition of "self" and affirming that "Blackness" contained multiple subject positions. This reaffirms the fact that Blackness can be defined from multiple perspectives. De La Soul assumed this posture for their first album, *3 Feet High and Rising.* On their second album they boldly declared that "De La Is Dead," short-circuiting the continuation of this style of rap.

6. The definition of function regarding African American lips in the larger culture can be seen in two recent cinematic examples. Use of the close-up and emphasis on the lips as derogatory stereotype occur in the repeated shots of the African American female radio announcer in the Walter Hill film *The Warriors* (1979). Though the character offers exterior commentary on the plight of the main characters, the street gang the Warriors, as they proceed along the narrative's mysterious path, this character has no identity; she is reduced to her function without recourse to any sustained narrative or visual involvement other than these repeated tight shots that emphasize her "nigger lips."

More recently, and in contrast to the earlier example, this tight shot of the lips was utilized in Spike Lee's *Do the Right Thing* (1989) with the character of Mr. Señor Love Daddy. In this case, the emphasis on lips becomes an example of the bodily vehicle for the oral tradition. While also functioning as the voice of exterior commentary, Love Daddy is able to articulate the film's rational direction from his empowered position and is also used as a voice of reason in relation to the societal conflicts presented in this film. In addition, Love Daddy connects the film to its oral roots when he engages in a roll call of prominent African American musical figures, both past and present. This use of the lips as vehicle for the oral tradition is also referenced repeatedly throughout *Mo Better Blues* (1990). The film's main character, Bleek Gillam, is shown as being obsessed with his lips as they determine his professional and emotional stability, especially when connected with the jazz that emerges from his trumpet.

Arrested Development's use of this racial trope can be seen as an extension of Mr. Señor Love Daddy and Bleek's function as oral facilitators within the Spike Lee films. This racial trope is also an embrace of the Africanness of their bodily features, and in turn a rejection of the traditionally Eurocentric standards of beauty in American society. Much like the often-mentioned griot of African society, the lips as visual metaphor, emphasized through extreme close-up in this case, become very useful in exemplifying the oral nature of African American culture. Also, the critique of dominant standards of beauty, at both white and African American levels, can be seen in the group's most prominent female character, who sports a bald head. While Irish female singer Sinead O'Connor is the most visible example of this style in popular white culture, the female participant in Arrested Development uses this stylistic device to affirm the group's Afrocentric cultural project.

A Small Introduction to the "G" Funk Era

THREE

1. There is another interesting exploration of this subject in Robin Kelly's "Kickin Reality, Kickin Ballistics: Gangsta Rap and Postindustrial Los Angeles." While Kelly covers some of the same terrain, his argument attempts to resurrect a political image of gangsta rap, while seemingly denouncing as regressive most of the material that does not fit into his discussion. A rejection of Snoop Doggy Dogg's presence at the conclusion of his essay is indicative of this strategy. It is my argument that the overwhelming majority of gangsta rap is defined by the rejection of politics that Kelly castigates; thus I am more interested in these overt rejections that have evolved in the genre and eventually made it the major market commodity that it is, especially post–Ice Cube.

2. For a lengthy discussion of the "bad nigga," see Lawrence Levine's *Black Culture and Black Consciousness* and Charles Henry's *Culture and African American Politics*. For a discussion of the recurrence of this image in contemporary popular culture, see my "The Day the Niggaz Took Over."

3. Though Tricia Rose's *Black Noise* is an important contribution to the discussion of rap music, one of the central problems with the book, for me, is its view of New York as the exclusive center of rap as a discursive form. While this was true in the 1980s, West Coast rap has transformed the medium since that time in both cultural impact and record sales. Gangsta rap made rap into the mainstream force it is today. Thus, my focus here is on the specificity of West Coast rap as creating its own discourse and ultimately influencing and forcing the East Coast to reconsider its one-time dominance in the rap industry.

4. For a further discussion of the differences between East Coast and West Coast style in rap music, see my article "The Geography of Style."

Young, Black, and Don't Give a Fuck

FOUR

1. The popular 1990 Martin Scorsese film *Goodfellas* is different from the gangster films which preceded it. At the conclusion of this film, the main character, Henry Hill, turns state's evidence on his former colleagues, thus violating one of the most stringent codes of the gangster lifestyle. And though some would argue that this film is a revisionist gangster film, it is sufficiently separated from other examples of the genre so as not to be confused. Scorsese's *Casino* (1995) continues this move to a contemporary gangster epic.

Another example of this revisionist trend would be Barry Levinson's fictional account of the life of Benjamin "Bugsy" Segal, with its emphasis on Segal's mistress, Virginia Hill, and the way in which her influence can be read as substantial, though detrimental, to Segal in the financial decisions that he makes. *Bugsy* (1991) presents a sentimental underworld figure who has been "softened" by this female presence, which goes against the masculinist approach normally associated with the gangster. This rereading of the central character, with an emphasis on the female, adds to my notion of a revisionist trend in the genre, though in this case it is gender, not race, that is the point of transition.

2. For a detailed discussion of the drug trade in Los Angeles, see Mike Davis, "The Political Economy of Crack," in *City of Quartz,* and for a larger discussion of the role played by the media, the politics of Reagan/Bush, and the drug culture of the 1980s, see Jimmie Reeves and Richard Campbell, *Cracked Coverage* (1993).

True to the Game

FIVE

1. In addition, another character who happens to encourage Buggin' Out's frustration wears a Magic Johnson jersey, clearly putting into dialogue the cultural standing of the game's three most important contemporary players, Magic, Bird, and Jordan.

2. Recently Magic Johnson and Isiah Thomas have gained small shares of the Lakers and Toronto Raptors, respectively. In the late 1980s there was a bid by an African American group, led by Peter Bynoe, to purchase the Denver Nuggets, but the deal ultimately fell through.

3. For an extended discussion of the "formal and the vernacular," see the liner notes to Robert Hurst's *One for Namesake* (DIW/Columbia Music, 1994).

4. For a more extensive discussion of Jordan the basketball player and pop cultural icon, see John Edgar Wideman, "Michael Jordan Leaps the Great Divide"; Susan Willis, "I Want the Black One: Is There a Place for Afro-American Culture in Commodity Culture?"; Michael Dyson, *Reflecting Black*; Sam Smith, *The Jordan Rules*; Bob Greene, *Hang Time*; Mitchell Krugel, *Jordan: The Man, His Words, His Life*; and Jordan's own photobiography, Mark Vancil's *Rare Air.*

5. For a detailed discussion of the Celtics' history of racial politics, see Harvey Araton and Filip Bondy, *The Selling of the Green: The Financial Rise and the Moral Decline of the Boston Celtics.*

6. I would be remiss if I did not mention the popularity of football in African American culture. It is this popularity that made O.J. Simpson the first significant Black celebrity endorser during the 1970s, long before he would be accused of killing his ex-wife and Ronald Goldman. Yet football, though immensely popular, especially at the high school and college level, has yet to articulate a significant Black aesthetic on the level of basketball. As certain positions on the football field are still occupied almost exclusively by white players, positions such as quarterback, which can have a substantial impact on the production of meaning, relative to style, the overwhelming contributions of Blacks remain somewhat restrained. Suffice it to say that all sports that African

Americans have played exhibit to some extent the culturally distinct style of Black culture, but basketball is the place where this has been done most obviously.

7. A more detailed account of Rodman's exploits appears in his popular book *As Bad As I Wanna Be* (with Jim Keown; Delacorte Press, 1996).

Works Cited

Araton, Harvey, and Filip Bondy. *The Selling of the Green: The Financial Rise and the Moral Decline of the Boston Celtics.* New York: Harper Collins, 1992.

Asante, Molefi. *Afrocentricity.* Trenton: Africa World Press, 1988.

Bakeer, Donald. *Crips: The Story of the South Central L.A. Street Gang from 1971– 1985.* Los Angeles: Precocious Publishing, 1992.

Baker, Houston, Jr. *Blues, Ideology and Afro American Literature: A Vernacular Theory.* Chicago: University of Chicago Press, 1984.

———. *Rap Music, Black Studies, and the Academy.* Chicago: University of Chicago Press, 1993.

Baudrillard, Jean. *Selected Writings.* Edited by Mark Poster. Stanford: Stanford University Press, 1988.

———. *Simulations.* New York: Columbia University Press, 1983.

Berube, Michael. "Public Academy." *The New Yorker,* January 9, 1995, pp. 73– 80.

Boyd, Todd. "Check Yo Self, Before You Wreck Yo Self: Variations on a Political Theme in Rap Music and Popular Culture." *Public Culture* 7, no. 1 (Autumn 1994): 1–23.

———. "The Day the Niggaz Took Over: Basketball, Commodity Culture, and Black Masculinity." In Aaron Baker and Todd Boyd, eds., *Out of Bounds: Sports, Media, and the Politics of Identity.* Bloomington: Indiana University Press (forthcoming).

———. "The Geography of Style: Rap Wages a Bicoastal Battle over the Nation's Hearts, Minds, and Ears." *Chicago Tribune,* October 2, 1994, pp. 33–34.

———. "The Meaning of the Blues." *Wide Angle* 13, nos. 3–4 (1991): 56–61.

———. "Popular Culture and Political Empowerment." *Cineaste* XIX, no. 1 (1993): 12–13.

———. "Tarantino's Mantra?" *Chicago Tribune,* November 6, 1994, p. 26.

Boyton, Robert. "The New Intellectuals." *The Atlantic Monthly,* March 1995, pp. 53–70.

Brown, Elaine. *A Taste of Power: A Black Woman's Story.* New York: Pantheon, 1992.

Carter, Stephen L. *Reflections of an Affirmative Action Baby.* New York: Basic Books, 1991.

Cleage, Albert. *The Black Messiah.* New York: Sheed and Ward, 1968.

Cone, James. *Black Theology: A Documentary History.* New York: Orbis Books, 1993.

Cose, Ellis. *The Rage of a Privileged Class.* New York: Harper Collins, 1993.

Cross, Brian. *It's Not about a Salary: Rap, Race, and Resistance in Los Angeles.* New York and London: Verso Press, 1993.

Crouch, Stanley. *Notes of a Hanging Judge: Essays and Reviews, 1979–1989.* New York: Oxford University Press, 1990.

Davis, Mike. *City of Quartz: Excavating the Future in Los Angeles.* New York and London: Verso Press, 1990.

Debord, Guy. *The Society of the Spectacle.* Detroit: Black and Red Press, 1983.

Dent, Gina, ed. *Black Popular Culture.* Seattle: Bay Press, 1993.

Diehl, Digby. "Michael Jordan." *Playboy,* May 1992, pp. 51, 63.

Du Bois, W. E. B. *The Souls of Black Folk.* New York: Knopf, 1993.

Dyson, Michael. *Making Malcolm: The Myth and Meaning of Malcolm X.* New York: Oxford University Press, 1995.

———. *Reflecting Black.* Minneapolis: University of Minnesota Press, 1993.

Ellis, Trey. *Home Repairs.* New York: Simon and Schuster, 1993.

———. "The New Black Aesthetic." *Before Columbus Review,* May 15, 1989, pp. 4, 23.

———. *Platitudes.* New York: Vintage Books, 1988.

Ellison, Ralph. *Invisible Man.* New York: Modern Library, 1992.

Fanon, Frantz. *The Wretched of the Earth.* Translated by Constance Farrington. New York: Grove Press, 1968.

Fuller, Hoyt. "Towards a Black Aesthetic." In *The Black Aesthetic,* ed. Addison Gayle. New York: Doubleday Press, 1971.

Fulwood, Sam III. "Intellectuals in the Promised Land." *Los Angeles Times Magazine,* April 9, 1995, pp. 10–14, 29–33.

Gates, Henry Louis, Jr. "Blood Brothers: Albert and Allen Hughes in the Belly of the Hollywood Beast." *Transition* 63 (1994): 164–77.

Gayle, Addison, ed. *The Black Aesthetic.* New York: Doubleday Press, 1971.

George, Lynell. *No Crystal Stair: African Americans in the City of Angels.* New York: Anchor Press, 1992.

George, Nelson. *Buppies, B-Boys, BAPS, and Bohos.* New York: Harper Collins Publishers, 1992.

———. *Elevating The Game.* New York: Harper Collins Publishers, 1992.

Gilroy, Paul. "After the Love Has Gone": Bio-politics and Etho-poetics in the Black Public Sphere." *Public Culture* 7, no. 1 (Fall 1994): 49–76.

Goines, Donald. *Dope Fiend.* Los Angeles: Holloway House Publishing Company, 1971.

———. *WhoreSon.* Los Angeles: Holloway House Publishing Company, 1972.

Gordone, Charles. *No Place to Be Somebody: A Black Black Comedy in Three Acts.* Indianapolis: Bobbs-Merrill, 1969.

Gray, Herman. "Television, Black Americans, and the American Dream." *Critical Studies in Mass Communication* 6 (1989): 376–86.

Greene, Bob. *Hang Time: Days and Dreams with Michael Jordan.* New York: St. Martin's Press, 1993.

Guerrero, Ed. *Framing Blackness.* Philadelphia: Temple University Press, 1993.

Henry, Charles. *Culture and African American Politics.* Bloomington: Indiana University Press, 1990.

Himes, Chester. *Cotton Comes to Harlem.* Chatham, N.J.: Hatham Bookseller, 1975.

hooks, bell. *Black Looks: Race and Representation.* Boston: South End Press, 1992.

———. *Outlaw Culture: Resisting Representation.* New York: Routledge, 1994.

hooks, bell, and Cornel West. *Breaking Bread: Insurgent Black Intellectual Life.* Boston: South End Press, 1991.

Jhally, Sut, and Justin Lewis. *Enlightened Racism: The Cosby Show, Audiences, and the Myth of the American Dream.* Boulder: Westview Press, 1992.

Jones, Leroi (Amiri Baraka). *The Dutchman and the Slave.* New York: William Morrow, 1964.

Jones, Lisa. *Bulletproof Diva.* New York: Doubleday, 1994.

Junod, Tom. "Can Grant Hill Save Sports?" *GQ,* April 1995, pp. 170–75, 238–40.

Kelly, Robin. "Kickin Reality, Kickin Ballistics: Gangsta Rap and Postindustrial Los Angeles." In *Race Rebels: Culture, Politics and the Black Working Class.* New York: Free Press, 1994.

Krugel, Mitchell. *Jordan: The Man, His Words, His Life.* New York: St. Martin's Press, 1993.

Lamar, Jake. *Bourgeois Blues: An American Memoir.* New York: Summit Books, 1991.

Lee, Spike, with Ralph Wiley. *By Any Means Necessary: The Trials and Tribulations of Making* Malcolm X. New York: Hyperion, 1992.

Les, Gene. *Cats of Many Colors.* New York: Oxford University Press, 1994.

Levine, Lawrence. *Black Culture and Black Consciousness.* New York: Oxford University Press, 1977.

Locke, Alain. *The New Negro.* New York: Atheneum Press, 1986.

Madhubuti, Haki. *Black Men: Obsolete, Single and Dangerous? African American Families in Transition: Essays in Discovery, Solution and Hope.* Chicago: Third World Press, 1990.

McCall, Nathan. *Make Me Wanna Holler: A Young Black Man in America.* New York: Random House, 1994.

Mercer, Kobena. "Black Hair/Style Politics." In *Out There: Marginalization and Contemporary Cultures,* ed. Russell Ferguson, Martha Gever, Trinh T. Minh-ha, and Cornel West. New York and Cambridge: The New Museum of Contemporary Art and MIT Press, 1990.

Monster Kody. *See* Shakur, Sanyika.

Mosley, Walter. *Black Betty.* New York: Norton, 1994.

———. *Devil in a Blue Dress.* New York: Norton, 1990.

———. *White Butterfly.* New York: Norton, 1992.

Muhammed, Elijah. *Message to the Black Man.*

Murray, Albert. *Stomping the Blues.* New York: McGraw Hill, 1976.

Nelson, Jill. *Volunteer Slavery: My Authentic Negro Experience.* Chicago: Nelson Press, 1993.

Pulley, Brett. "How a Nice Girl Evolved into Boss, the Gangster Rapper." *Wall Street Journal,* February 3, 1994, pp. A1–2, A10–11.

Reeves, Jimmie, and Richard Campbell. *Cracked Coverage.* Durham: Duke University Press, 1994.

Rose, Tricia. *Black Noise: Rap Music and Black Culture in Contemporary America.* Boston: University Press of New England, 1994.

————. "Never Trust a Big Butt and a Smile." *Camera Obscura* 23 (1990).

Shakur, Sanyika (aka Monster Kody). "Can't Stop, Won't Stop: The Education of a Crip Warlord." *Esquire,* April 1993, pp. 87–139.

————. *Monster: The Autobiography of an L.A. Gang Member.* Toronto: Penguin Books, 1993.

Silver, Michael. "Rodman Unchained." *Sports Illustrated,* May 29, 1995, pp. 20, 28.

Slim, Iceberg. *The Naked Soul of Iceberg Slim.* Los Angeles: Holloway House Publishing Company, 1971.

————. *Pimp: The Story of My Life.* Los Angeles: Holloway House Publishing Company, 1969.

————. *Trick Baby.* Los Angeles: Holloway House Publishing Company, 1967.

Smith, Sam. *The Jordan Rules.* New York: Pocket Books, 1993.

Steele, Shelby. *The Content of Our Character: A New Vision of Race in America.* New York: Harper Perennial, 1991.

Tate, Greg. *Flyboy in the Buttermilk.* New York: Fireside Press, 1992.

Taylor, Phil. "Bad Actors: The Growing Number of Selfish and Spoiled Players Are Hurting Their Teams and Marring the NBA's Image." *Sports Illustrated,* January 30, 1995, pp. 18–23.

Thomas, Greg. "Who's Winning the Black Studies War?" *The Village Voice,* January 17, 1995, pp. 23–29.

Vancil, Mark, ed. *Rare Air.* New York: Collins Publishers, 1993.

Wallace, Michelle. *Invisibility Blues: From Pop to Theory.* London: Verso Press, 1990.

————. "Making Monster." *Los Angeles Times Magazine,* April 4, 1993, pp. 16–56.

Washington, Booker T. *Up from Slavery.* New York: Dell Publishing, 1965.

West, Cornel. "The New Politics of Difference." In *Out There: Marginalization and Contemporary Cultures,* ed. Russell Ferguson, Martha Gever, Trinh T. Minh-ha, and Cornel West. New York and Cambridge: The New Museum of Contemporary Art and MIT Press, 1990.

————. *Race Matters.* Boston: Beacon Press, 1993.

Wideman, John Edgar. "Michael Jordan Leaps the Great Divide." *Esquire,* November 1990, pp. 141–210.

Willis, Susan. "I Want the Black One: Is There a Place for Afro- American Culture in Commodity Culture?" *New Formations* 10 (spring 1990): 77–97.

Wilson, August. *The Piano Lesson.* New York: Plume, 1990.

Wilson, William Julius. *The Truly Disadvantaged: The Inner City, The Underclass, and Public Policy.* Chicago: University of Chicago Press, 1987.

Woods, Joe, ed. *Malcolm X: In Our Own Image.* New York: St. Martin's Press, 1992.

Woodson, Carter G. *The Miseducation of the Negro.* Trenton, N.J.: Africa World Press, 1990.

Wright, Richard. *Native Son.* New York and London: Harper, 1941.

Index

TODD BOYD IS A
PROFESSOR AT THE SCHOOL
OF CINEMA-TELEVISION AT
THE UNIVERSITY OF SOUTHERN
CALIFORNIA. HE COEDITED
(WITH AARON BAKER) *OUT OF
BOUNDS: SPORTS, MEDIA, AND
THE POLITICS OF IDENTITY*. HE
HAS WRITTEN FOR THE *LOS
ANGELES TIMES* AND THE
CHICAGO TRIBUNE AND HAS
PUBLISHED ESSAYS IN A VARIETY
OF JOURNALS, INCLUDING
*PUBLIC CULTURE, SIGHT AND
SOUND, CINEASTE, WIDE ANGLE,
FILMFORUM, FILM QUARTERLY,*
AND *CINE 21* (SEOUL, KOREA).
HE ALSO WROTE THE LINER
NOTES FOR THE DISC OF THE
HUGHES BROTHERS' *MENACE II
SOCIETY* AND PROVIDED THE
VOICE-OVER COMMENTARY ON
THE CRITERION LASER DISC FOR
THE HUGHES BROTHERS' FILM
DEAD PRESIDENTS.

Riley